Do You Believe It?

Do You Believe It?

A Guide to a Reasonable Christian Faith

Peter Harris

WIPF & STOCK · Eugene, Oregon

DO YOU BELIEVE IT?
A Guide to a Reasonable Christian Faith

Wipf & Stock
An Imprint of Wipf and Stock Publishers
199 W. 8th Ave., Suite 3
Eugene, OR 97401

www.wipfandstock.com

PAPERBACK ISBN: 978-1-7252-5616-3
HARDCOVER ISBN: 978-1-7252-5617-0
EBOOK ISBN: 978-1-7252-5618-7

Manufactured in the U.S.A.   02/24/21

This book is dedicated to Steve Bruce, David Johnson, Pastor Veyne Austin, and to the memory of Cyril Baker (1927–2014) and Ethel Baker (1921–2015). Thank you for helping to restore my Christian faith. It is dedicated also to the memory of Pastor Ray Bindra (1952–2016) who preached the Gospel to my whole family at my wedding.

Contents

Preface

WHEN I WAS A 19-year-old student, I rejected my Christian faith of seven years and lived as an atheist for eight years. I had made friends with a fellow student who was an atheist and he challenged me to prove my faith. What made my friend a great debater was that he had clearly thought very much about the issues we were debating and as he was studying philosophy, he knew many of the arguments against the existence of God. On the other hand, I had never been taught to defend my faith rationally and how to challenge the atheist worldview in turn. I decided to investigate atheism and read books by well-known skeptics such as Bertrand Russell and David Hume. Against their criticisms I had no response. I had no idea that there have been and are many robust defenders of the Christian faith. C. S. Lewis for me was the author of charming children's stories rather than the foremost apologist of the twentieth century. I had never even heard of Dorothy L. Sayers or Norman Geisler, let alone read their works. Deeply troubled by my weakening faith, I did something I would never ordinarily have done: I visited without prior arrangement one cold, somber Sunday evening an acquaintance of mine who was a Christian. He was studying science and seemed a very mature believer. I thought he was the one who could satisfy my doubts. Over a cup of tea I asked him to give me a knock-down reason for why I ought to be a Christian. He was surprised by the question and supplied me with the answer that I least wanted to hear: Being a Christian was a matter of simply believing it. There were no reasons. It was a matter of faith. Taking his response as the best Christianity could muster, my faith slowly died and I chose atheism.

I do not blame my acquaintance for my temporary departure from Christianity. He most likely did not know any arguments for Christianity either as he had never been taught them. He did his best to help me, but it was not enough. When I look back on this episode which happened just over thirty years ago, I am struck by the fact that I did not question more of my Christian friends and acquaintances. It was as if I had already made up my mind about Christianity and though my acquaintance's failure to provide an argument dismayed and angered me, it also confirmed what I had already concluded: That Christianity was superstition. I wanted to be considered an intellectual and remember thinking to myself that if I were to be regarded as such, I ought to become an atheist. Declaring myself to be an atheist excited me because it seemed daring. Both emotional and intellectual forces were therefore acting on my decision-making with the emotional forces pushing me into atheism and the intellectual forces confirming that choice.

Memories of this moment in my life have never left me. I remember it clearly and it has taught me the importance of knowing why we believe in Christ and how we may best help others who have doubts and those who have no faith, but who have challenged what we believe. If you have not yet questioned the truth of your faith, one day you might. If you have never been asked by another Christian for help during their doubting, one day you probably will. If people know you are a Christian, eventually someone will challenge what you believe. The aim of this book is to help sustain and strengthen your and others' faith. Its aim too is to enable you to answer some of the tough questions non-believers ask. I hope you enjoy it.

Acknowledgments

MANY THANKS GO TO Pastor David Webster and Father Michael Payne for inviting me to give seminars at the churches they lead which have featured some of the arguments in this book.

Introduction

HAVING QUESTIONS ABOUT THE truth of our faith and being questioned about our faith is something we should not worry about if we know where to find answers for our doubts and we have knowledgeable people with whom we can talk. Our and others' questions are wonderful opportunities to reflect on what we believe and to present the Gospel to unbelievers. The problem we face is that many Christians do not know how they will answer skeptical questions about their faith. This is not wholly their fault. We Christians live at a moment when emotions and sensations are given far more importance than reason and evidence within the Christian lifestyle. In the face of a powerful skepticism arising from that period of history in the eighteenth century called the Enlightenment, and which has continued today, many Christians turned Christianity into a religion of the heart rather than stand their intellectual ground. The effects of this are still with us. For example, I once attended a church service during which the speaker told us that so-called 'Greek' or logical ways of thinking are not as good as the 'Hebrew' way of thinking. The speaker did not explain what she meant by the Hebrew way of thinking, but as she was contrasting it with logical thinking, we can conclude that she meant that the Hebrews were somehow non-logical. The irony is that her rejection of logic requires us to think logically to understand it! Furthermore, she is ignorant of the occasions when Jesus used logic in His disputes with the Pharisees, Sadducees, and teachers of the law (see, for example, Matt. 12:10-14; 12:22-28; 16:13-20). It also makes you wonder how Solomon's architects

990-931 BCE.

Mathmatics — Sumerians
3000 Mesopotamia
B.C. complex system
earliest civilization

and engineers put up the Temple without the aid of mathematics. It is no surprise that much of the service was taken up with people expressing their emotions to God (a good thing), but little exercise of the mind was required (a bad thing). It was lullaby Christianity rather than grown-up Christianity that seeks to engage the mind as well as the heart.

This imbalance towards the heart is unusual because traditionally Christianity has been as much about the head as it is the heart. Johann Sebastian Bach wrote music in praise of God that can bring us to tears; Thomas Aquinas wrote philosophy over which we can think for a lifetime. We are meant to be whole, balanced people who love through the feelings we express, the acts we perform, and the thoughts that we share. Nevertheless, we have the reputation of being ignorant among our atheist opponents. The New Atheist Richard Dawkins defines Christians as people who are happy not to know about the world in which they live. Dawkins knows better than this because he has said that he knows biologists who have a Christian faith.[1] Of course, not all contemporary Christians are headless. There are many Christians who think about their faith and are interested in knowing its rational foundations as evidenced by the large numbers who attend apologetics conferences. But too many of our brothers and sisters appear not to want or need to know the evidence for what they believe. For them, to look for reasons for their beliefs seems like a 'lack of faith'. Some do not even know there is evidence for the Christian faith in the first place. This mirrors the world we live in. Hollywood, reality television, social media, the advertising industry, and electioneering politicians press our emotional buttons far more often than they do our thinking buttons. If our Christianity only gives us feelings and little thinking, we are in a dangerous place. It is our Christian reason guided and informed by Scripture that ought to enable us to step back and think critically about the culture we live in and keep our faith on track. We are called as Christians to create thinking and feeling communities devoted to God and one another in love where thought and emotion are held in the correct

1. Dawkins, "God Delusion' (Full Documentary)."

balance. We are called to love God with our minds (Mark 12:30, 33; Luke 10:27) which I take to mean that we are to love God by desiring to know Him better and to think of Him accurately as far as we can with our finite minds.

My book is offered to several audiences. First, to those who have questions and doubts about their faith. Second, to those who have been challenged as to why they believe in Jesus. And third, to those who see the importance of knowing why we believe and wish to help a doubting Christian or an inquiring skeptic. Though it is impossible to answer all the questions we might have, or be faced with during our earthly existence, there are nevertheless answers to many questions. Unless we know them, we will be troubled by them and our questioners, for whom we have no answer, will conclude that Christianity is an inadequate worldview

It is therefore no surprise that providing reasons for our faith is a command from God no less:

> But have reverence for Christ in your hearts and honor him as Lord. Be ready at all times to answer anyone who asks you to explain the hope you have in you but do it with gentleness and respect. Keep your conscience clear, so that when you are insulted, those who speak evil of your good conduct as followers of Christ will become ashamed of what they say' (1 Pet. 3:15-16).

These verses teach the truth that if we are to be effective witnesses for Christ, we need to know how to defend our Christian belief and our lifestyles need to be Christ-like. It is no good if we can give clever answers as to why Christianity is true when we are living bad lives, for our lives will undermine our answers. Equally, if we are living good lives which attract people to our beliefs, but we cannot give reasons for why we believe, our ignorance will undermine our witness. If our lives and thoughts are a testimony to the truth of Christianity, even though our enemies make up accusations against us, they will be put to shame. As we learn the excellent reasons for why we believe, may we pray to God that the quality of our lives will match the quality of our reasons.

This book aims first to provide a line of argument from the evidence for the Resurrection that demonstrates that Christianity is a reasonable worldview worthy of careful examination. The problem with the Resurrection argument for Christianity is that it suggests that God exists, but equally it could be argued that a superior being like a super angel raised Jesus from the dead. Therefore, we will explore what I call signposts to the divine. These are bits of information that are highly suggestive of the existence of God or gods. Third, we will close the gap between the argument for the Resurrection and the signposts to the divine by examining good reasons for thinking that the Triune God of Christianity was responsible for Jesus' Resurrection. In other words, it was God the Son who came as Jesus filled with God the Holy Spirit who died and was raised from the dead by God the Father. Finally, we will think about and answer questions on very significant contemporary issues which can be obstacles to faith. The aim is that your faith will stand strong in the face of doubt and that you can be an effective witness of your faith to doubters and unbelievers. It is important to emphasize that this book is a starting point for your own continued study of the matters concerned which I say without exaggeration can last a lifetime and maybe beyond! Therefore, I have provided you with further reading and a bibliography to which you may refer.

I have also included a discussion guide at the very end of the book which provides questions about the content of each of the chapters. The discussion guide is designed to be used by Christians with each other, by parents/guardians with their children, and ministers with their congregations to learn together how to advocate for the Christian faith. We can learn by reading a book which is a very pleasurable and effective way to learn. Yet this little book does not have all the answers. Far from it. But meeting with other Christians has the additional advantage of bringing together the wealth of knowledge and understanding that each possesses. We can pick each other's brains and work things out together.

The discussion guide is included for another very important reason: To encourage the Church to treat those with doubts in a kind and mature way. Some individual Christians and churches treat doubt as a shameful thing. They give no room in which people can express their doubts and seek answers. The writer, Philip Yancey, has written on his blog about how the church in which he grew up taught that doubts were to be ignored and because he hid his doubts, they remained unresolved and resulted in his rejecting his faith for a time.[2] The study guide is included in order to encourage churches to avoid the mistake of suppressing doubts and provide the safe space of discussion groups in which Christians with doubts can express them and receive non-judgmental, reasoned responses.

2. Yancey, "Faith and Doubt."

1

The Resurrection: An Excellent Place to Start

IF YOU WANT TO defend your faith and give reasons as to why others ought to share it, the Resurrection is an excellent place to start. Christianity lives or falls by the truth of the Resurrection of Jesus. No Resurrection=no Christian faith. Why? The apostle Paul explains it in this way:

> "Now since our message is that Christ has been raised from death, how can some of you say that the dead will not be raised to life? If that is true, it means that Christ was not raised; and if Christ has not been raised from death, then we have nothing to preach and you have nothing to believe. More than that, we are shown to be lying about God, because we said that he raised Christ from death-but if it is true that the dead are not raised to life, then he did not raise Christ. For if the dead are not raised, neither has Christ been raised. And if Christ has not been raised, then your faith is a delusion and you are still lost in your sins" (1 Cor. 15:12–17).

We are left in no doubt by Paul's logic that without the Resurrection, there is no Christianity. Paul's argument proceeds in steps and look like this: if p then q, if q then r and so on. Paul's writings are an important reminder that the proper use of logic is part of loving God with our minds. It is indeed not only a Greek way of thinking but a Hebrew way of thinking and a human/divine way of thinking too!

It is also worth pointing out that in the translation I am using, the *Good News Bible*, the word delusion is used. Christianity is a delusion, not because Richard Dawkins thinks so,[1] but if the Resurrection had not occurred!

Why is Paul able to declare so strongly that unless Jesus has risen from the dead, all Christian faith pointless? It is because Christianity is premised on the belief that Jesus is divine as well as human. The Gospels say that Jesus predicted his Resurrection. If Jesus' prediction was false and he did not rise, he could not have been divine for He would have been guilty of error. It therefore follows that if Jesus was not divine, He was not sinless and so could not have died for others' sin. The whole of Christianity is at stake if the Resurrection is not true. Thankfully, it is possible to look at the historical sources and conclude reasonably that the best explanation for the birth of the Church is that Jesus did indeed rise from the dead.

The Minimal Facts Approach

We can strengthen our faith and appeal to skeptics through what is called the 'Minimal Facts Approach' to the Resurrection. It is an approach that has been pioneered by a leading Christian scholar of the Resurrection, Gary Habermas. Rather than attempt to convince skeptics that the New Testament is a true historical record (which it is), the Minimal Facts Approach takes the historical events for which there is strong evidence and which are accepted by nearly all scholars in the field, including the harshest skeptics.[2] It then uses these facts and supporting facts to demonstrate that the best explanation for the Resurrection is that Jesus did rise from the dead. If you use this method, it will enable you to avoid being diverted by skeptics into debates over whether the New Testament

1. The book that made Dawkins' name as a New Atheist is *The God Delusion*.

2. Habermas and Licona, *The Case for the Resurrection*, 47.

is historically true and will enable you to keep their focus on the question, did Jesus rise from the dead?[3]

You may have noticed that I have added the word bodily to the word resurrection in the above sentence. The reason for this is that you may have come across the argument that Jesus rose from the dead spiritually but not physically. The Bible, however, teaches that Jesus' body was raised too. During our discussion of the Resurrection, I will address the "no-body" theory of the Resurrection and why we should not accept it.

The Twelve Facts Accepted by Many Scholars

Habermas has listed the following twelve as accepted by many scholars as historical facts:

1. **Jesus died by being crucified.**

2. Jesus was buried.

3. The disciples were demoralized by Jesus' death because they believed He was dead and had no belief He would rise.

4. **A few days later, Jesus' tomb was found to be empty.**

5. **The disciples had experiences they believed were of the resurrected Jesus.**

6. The experiences transformed the disciples into bold proclaimers of Jesus' Resurrection.

7. The Early Church made the Resurrection its foundational belief.

8. Jesus died in Jerusalem and the Resurrection was first proclaimed in Jerusalem.

9. The Church grew as a result of this preaching.

10. Sunday became the day of worship even though the first believers were Jews who celebrated the Sabbath from Friday sunset to Saturday sunset.

3. Ibid., 45.

11. **James, Jesus' brother, was an unbeliever, but became a believer.**

12. **Paul was converted after seeing what he thought was the resurrected Jesus.**[4]

Habermas and his co-writer, Michael Licona, however, do not need to use all twelve facts. Remember, their approach is to use the minimal number of facts required to build the case for the Resurrection. Habermas and Licona therefore only use five which have been highlighted by being typed in bold above.[5] Facts one, five, eleven and twelve are accepted as true by nearly all scholars and fact four is supported by an impressive number of scholars.[6]

Natural Explanations for the Resurrection

In order to show that the Resurrection of Jesus is the best explanation for what happened at the first Easter, it is necessary to know what natural explanations have been given and why they fail to fit the five facts. There are twelve alternative theories:

Empty Tomb Theory One: Without the disciples' knowledge, Jesus' body was buried in a mass grave, so the tomb where they thought Jesus had been buried was empty and this led to their belief He had risen from the dead.

Empty Tomb Theory Two: The women, grieving and confused, went to the wrong tomb, found it empty and mistakenly told the other disciples that Jesus had come back to life.

Legend Theory: The story of the Resurrection was initially a made-up story which over time was inflated to turn a charismatic sect leader into a divine figure.

Twin Theory: After Jesus had died, his identical twin-brother turned up in Jerusalem, was mistaken for Jesus and was worshipped as the risen Jesus.

4. Habermas, *The Historical Jesus*, 158–67.
5. Habermas and Licona, *The Case for the Resurrection*, 48–77.
6. Ibid., 48.

Hallucination Theory: The disciples thought they had seen the risen Jesus, but in fact they were hallucinating.

Existential Resurrection Theory: Jesus is dead, but that does not matter as the Christ of faith has risen in our hearts.

Spiritual Resurrection Theory: It was Jesus' spirit that rose from the dead, not his body.

Theft Theory: The disciples stole the body and claimed Jesus had returned to life.

Hidden Body Theory: The authorities hid Jesus' body, presumably to prevent the disciples from stealing it and claiming that Jesus was alive.

Swoon Theory: Jesus swooned (fainted) on the cross, and as he appeared to be dead, was buried. Whilst in the cool, quiet tomb, Jesus revived.

Passover Plot: Jesus planned to fulfil the Old Testament prophecies through a mock death and resurrection. The plot failed when Jesus was stabbed by a Roman soldier with a spear. A mysterious young man who happened to be on the scene at the time was mistaken for the risen Jesus.

Alien Theory: Jesus is an alien able to overcome death or appear dead.[7]

The Glass Slipper Technique

Now that we have had a chance to look at the minimal five facts and the attempts to explain the Resurrection away as a natural phenomenon, it is time to explore whether all the five facts can all fit into any of the explanations. It is Habermas' thesis that no natural explanation can contain all the facts and therefore no natural explanation can explain the Resurrection. The exception to this is the view that Jesus was an alien, but there are problems with this view as we shall see. Like Prince Charming looking for the lady whose foot will perfectly fit the shoe, so we are looking for the perfect fit of

7. Hazen, "Evidence for the Resurrection," Module One Lecture for Biola University's Certificate in Apologetics. To access the lecture, a person must be a student taking the Certificate in Apologetics.

facts to explanation. Like Prince Charming also, we will take each explanatory foot in turn and try it for size. Only the Cinderella of explanations, the supernatural one, is the perfect fit.

Facts and Theories

Empty tomb theory one is contradicted by fact four: That Jesus was buried in a tomb that was found to be empty. Even if Jesus had been buried in a mass grave without His disciples' knowledge, those who had buried him knew where he was. It would have been easy for Jesus' opponents to disprove the claims that Jesus was alive by presenting the body. There is no evidence that they did. Moreover, how long would the disciples go on believing that Jesus had risen from the dead if they had found an empty tomb and yet never saw him again? Why would James and Paul become Christians on the basis of an empty tomb? To James and Paul's skeptical minds, the best explanation would not have been a resurrection.

Empty tomb theory two cannot account for facts eleven and twelve. Even if the female disciples had gone to the wrong tomb and testified mistakenly that Jesus had risen, neither James nor Paul would have trusted the testimonies of women in an age when women's testimony was regarded as worthless. Their conversion therefore must be explained in another way.

Were the Resurrection narratives legends that accrued over time? For a legend to develop, usually there must be a time lapse between the event or the life of the person in question and the legend's emergence. Facts five, eleven and twelve wreck this theory. The first disciples had experiences of Jesus as the Risen Lord very soon after his death. James and Paul were among Jesus' contemporaries to testify he rose. The claim that Jesus had risen from the dead was made almost immediately after his death, not made up centuries later. It has been argued that legends grew up about Jesus during his life. That is conceivable as legends grew up about Alexander the Great, the ancient ruler of Macedon, Greece, and Persia, being divine during his lifetime. But if the belief in his Resurrection was part of a legend, why would James and Paul convert? James was a doubter regarding his brother Jesus (John 7:3–5) and Paul was a persecutor of Christians (Acts 9:1, 2). Neither man was in any way predisposed to accept legends about a man they believed was only a man.

It has been asserted that people mistook Jesus for his twin brother,[8] but this thesis has few supporters. In terms of our five facts, it clearly runs aground on fact eleven. James, the brother of Jesus, believed in the Resurrection of Jesus. It is very unlikely that James would have misidentified Jesus' twin brother for Jesus, even if he had never met that twin brother before.

The hallucination theory claims the disciples hallucinated that Jesus was alive. This looks possible as it is a common phenomenon for people to hallucinate dead people over whom they are deeply grieving (post-bereavement hallucination experiences or PBHEs). Surely the disciples would have been prone to these hallucinations because of their love for Jesus?

The hallucination theory cannot account for Paul's conversion. Before he became a Christian, Paul was certainly not grieving over Jesus' death (Acts 8:1–3). Whatever Paul saw, it was not an hallucination of Jesus caused by a traumatic sense of bereavement.

To explain away Paul's conversion, the New Atheist journalist, Christopher Hitchens, supposes that Paul's vision was due to epilepsy.[9] Epileptics certainly can have visions during their seizures, but there is a decisive problem with this view. It fails to explain the complete change in Paul's life from being a persecutor of Christianity to one of its most important apostles. The Russian novelist Dostoyevsky, who suffered from epilepsy, wrote of how deeply his visions enhanced his spiritual understanding, but they did not convert him out of his Christian beliefs: they reinforced them. Contemporary neuroscience confirms this. When Wilder Penfield conducted experiments in which he stimulated the temporal lobe which is responsible for epileptic fits, he found that not all his human subjects had religious experiences. Those who

8. See Robert Greg Cavin's PhD dissertation "Miracles, Probability, and the Resurrection of Jesus" for an excellent example of this line of argument.

9. Hitchens, *God is Not Great*, 5.

did described their religious experiences in terms of pre-existing religious beliefs in the way that Dostoyevsky did.[10] Paul, on the other hand, underwent a complete transformation of his intellect, will, and emotions. His whole worldview dramatically changed.[11] If Paul had been an epileptic, his hallucinations would have confirmed his Judaism rather than overturned it.

The existential resurrection theory avoids what its proponents regard as the embarrassment of asserting a miracle in a skeptical age, but it retains the belief in the risen Jesus as an emotional fact. According to this view, Jesus indeed died and remained dead, but the disciples 'resurrected' Jesus by keeping his memory alive and we can do the same too. Perhaps the risen Jesus is a symbol of human hope in goodness' ability to overcome evil?

But if we want hope, surely we would prefer a person who gives us hope rather than a symbol? Fortunately, the resurrected Jesus is not a symbol of hope, but the greatest source of hope because he is an historical person, both God and a man. The problem with the existential theory is that it cannot explain the fact of the empty tomb. If Jesus is only alive in our hearts, his body must be in the tomb. Before he became a Christian, Paul would not have had any sentimental allegiance to Jesus. Paul converted to Christianity, not because he treasured the memory of Jesus in his heart, but because he believed he saw Jesus alive. The existentialist therefore has the burden or responsibility of proof in explaining how a fanatical opponent of Christianity would convert to Christianity.

The spiritual resurrection theory claims that Jesus rose spiritually but not physically also. It is easier for some to say that a spirit survives death than to claim a body resurrects, but for full-blooded skeptics both propositions are ridiculous, so any attempt to impress skeptics with this will not work. The spiritual resurrection theory breaks on the rock of the empty tomb. If Jesus had risen spiritually, His body would still have been lying there, surely? It has been proposed that Jesus' body was moved. Therefore, we now turn to the two versions of this hypothesis.

10. Dirckx, *Am I Just My Brain?*, 107.

11. Bruce, *The Book of the Acts*, 183.

The theft theory claims that the disciples stole the body and then claimed Jesus had come back to life. This theory paints the disciples as fraudsters. The problem is fact five. The disciples could not have had experiences of what they truly believed was the risen Jesus if they knew for certain that Jesus was dead. To assert that Jesus was alive was a dangerous thing to do. Prominent witnesses to the Resurrection, such as James, Peter, and Paul, were martyred for their Christianity. It is unlikely that Peter, who would have been one of those who stole the body, would have suffered death for a con trick. James and Paul would not have converted either if they had sensed a fraud.

The hidden body theory asserts that the Sanhedrin (the rulers of Israel who had goaded the Romans into killing Jesus) hid the body to prevent the disciples from stealing it and claiming that Jesus had returned. But the problem with this is that Paul, who acted on the Sanhedrin's behalf against the Church (Acts 9:1, 2), would probably have known about it. Yet Paul converted to Christianity upon seeing what he thought was the Risen Christ.

The swoon theory accepts fact one, that Jesus was crucified, but fails because of that fact. As Jesus was crucified, it is highly improbable that he survived. Crucifixion was renowned for the destruction it wrought on the victim's body. To have a chance of survival, Jesus would have needed intensive medical care that only a modern hospital could give. Because crucifixion was reserved for traitors and the most dangerous of criminals, when someone was sentenced to be crucified the only outcome was death. Even the liberal New Testament scholar, John Dominic Crossan, is of the opinion that Jesus' death by crucifixion is as certain as any other historical fact.[12]

The Passover Plot is a type of conspiracy theory. There are many problems with this theory. The Passover Plot conspiracy agrees with fact one that Jesus was crucified. But why would a con-artist put himself through the agonies of crucifixion? Moreover, as we noted with the Swoon Theory, no one sentenced to crucifixion was meant to survive because of the dangerous nature of those condemned.

12. Crossan, *Jesus: A Revolutionary Biography*, 145.

As Cicero, the Roman politician and writer stated, crucifixion was a very cruel and humiliating death.[13] Jesus would have known this as he lived in a country where crucifixion was practiced. Would he therefore not have faked his death in a painless or a much less painful way that ran no or few risks for him?

Fact four refutes the Passover Plot. As Jesus was dead, his corpse would have been in the tomb, so why was His tomb empty? One way in which the Passover Plot seeks to explain this is to suggest that a mysterious young man was mistaken for Jesus. The problem with this idea is that James, Jesus' brother, became a believer and he would not have mistaken this mysterious young man for his brother.

Aliens are a popular figure in contemporary films and books. The Internet presents people who claim to have contact with them. As far as I can tell, no one who claims to have had contact with aliens has ever said that an alien has offered to die for the sins of humanity and promised to rise again. The scientific search for extraterrestrial life through the SETI project has found no evidence that such life exists. The theory that Jesus was an alien is consistent with all the facts, but that is because Jesus was an alien! Not in the sense of being one of the creatures that people claim to be abducted by, but because He was the God the Son who incarnated in a world fallen into sin.

The Slipper Fits!

The only theory that is left standing is that Jesus did rise from the dead. It is the foot that fits the slipper. It is consistent with not only the five minimal facts that Habermas and Licona use but with all the twelve facts. For Jesus to rise again, he would have to be dead, of course (fact one). That Jesus was buried (fact two) means that those who did the burying, which would have been people sympathetic to him as crucified victims were not dignified with burial, knew where the tomb was and were unlikely to mistake an unused

13. Cicero, *Against Verres*, 2.5.165.

tomb as an empty tomb. When the tomb was discovered to be empty (fact four), it was indeed Jesus' tomb. The disciples' demoralization at Jesus' death (fact three) required something extraordinary to happen for them to become bold proclaimers of Jesus' Resurrection (fact six). What turned the despairing disciples into courageous evangelists is their witnessing what they believed to be the resurrected Jesus (fact five). The best source of such certainty is that they did indeed see the risen Jesus. Seeing Jesus for real also best explains why the disciples had the valor to preach their message in the very city where Jesus had been crucified, where the Sanhedrin responsible for his death lived and where Pilate had his base (fact nine). It is also the best explanation for fact seven: That the Early Church made the Resurrection its foundational belief. The Jews did not expect the resurrection to happen before Judgement Day and the Greeks and the Romans scoffed at the idea of resurrection. The disciples had to be very certain that they had seen the living Jesus to make resurrection so central to their faith. What better reasons could there be than that they saw Jesus for real? That these first Jewish believers chose to change their Sabbath to Sunday is consistent also with their having seen the risen Jesus (fact ten). Fact nine says that the Church grew as a result of the disciples preaching that Jesus had risen. It is very difficult to explain how a small group of disciples who made the seemingly preposterous claim that a crucified man had come back to life could have captured the hearts of disbelieving crowds unless there was utter conviction in their demeanor. It would have taken a miracle such as a resurrection for the residents of and pilgrims in Jerusalem, and James and Paul, to have become followers of Jesus.

The Skeptic's Furthest Reach

But bringing a skeptic this far does not mean that s/he will believe in the risen Jesus. One thing a skeptic might say is what the scholar, Bart Ehrman, concludes: It is true that Jesus' followers, including Paul, had experiences that led them to conclude that Jesus was alive again, but what caused those experiences is unknown.[14] To be able to bring a skeptic thus far reveals how impressive the case for the Resurrection is, but Ehrman's position obviously stops short of accepting the supernatural explanation. It is at this point that Ehrman's naturalism decides the issue. If the supernatural does not exist, there must be a natural reason for what happened at the first Easter, it is just the case that we have not yet found it. Those who hold this position seem to suffer from the atheist's equivalent of the God of the gaps explanation: the naturalistic explanation of the gaps. Fortunately, it is possible to present the case for the existence of Christianity's God and that it was God the Father who raised Jesus. To provide further evidence, I shall turn to science.

14. Ehrman, *Jesus: Apocalyptic Prophet*, 230.

2

Signposts to God

The Relationship between Science and Christianity

WHEN I WAS AN undergraduate back in the late eighties, my view was that science and Christianity were enemies, primarily because of the theory of evolution. Science has disproved religion seemed to be science's boast. My school's biology teacher's skepticism seemed to prove the point. I was aware of one scientist who was a Christian called Victor Pearce who used scientific knowledge to demonstrate the Bible was true, but he was the only scientist I knew who was doing this. On entering university I made the acquaintance of several very talented science undergraduates who were Christians. This intrigued me and when I asked one of them how it was possible to be a Christian and a scientist, he said he was studying the handiwork of God. That certainly gave me pause for thought.

Nevertheless, the idea that Christianity and science are incompatible has been hard for me to shake off. This view has recently been reinforced for many by the books of New Atheism. Dawkins presents science and religion as complete opposites, with science on one side as the height of reason and religion on the other as the depth of irrationality. The Oxford chemist, Peter Atkins, thinks that religion is for people with lazy minds.[1]

The problem with these views is that they are simplistic. They make good soundbites in an age of short attention spans and are effective in rallying New Atheism's foot soldiers, but accurate

1. Premier Radio, "Unbelievable? John Lennox vs Peter Atkins—Can Science Explain Everything? Live Debate."

scholarship they are not. The experts in this field, namely histo-rians and sociologists of science, present a radically different and far subtler picture than the noisy New Atheists. R. K. Merton, a sociologist, has come up with the widely-accepted Merton Thesis which says that the rise of modern science was *assisted by Puritan values of the seventeenth century.*[2] (I have put those words in italics as you may wish to read them again and if there is any doubt, the Puritans were part of the Protestant Church.) Peter Harrison, who holds the Chair of Science and Religion at Oxford University, ar-gues that Protestant methods of interpreting the Bible stimulated scientific inquiry.[3] The historian of science, John Hedley Brooke, sees the relationship between religion and science as existing in three ways: conflict, complementarity and interrelationship.[4] Yes, there has been conflict between science and religion, but to say that that is the only relationship that has existed is untrue. The mathematician and philosopher, A. N. Whitehead, hypothesized that science emerged from the expectation that the universe is an ordered place, a view that came out of medieval theology's belief in a rational creator.[5] Someone might say to you that these emi-nent scholars and thinkers are probably Christians who allow their worldview to color their conclusions. I am not aware of the reli-gious opinions of Merton, Harrison, and Brooke. Whitehead did believe there was a God, but he was not a Christian. But why does having a Christian belief-system therefore mean that a scholar will be biased as s/he goes about his or her work? And are Mer-ton, Harrison, and Brooke not established scholars in their field regardless of their personal beliefs? And are Dawkins and Atkins not also open to the same charge that their atheist worldview is coloring their conclusions about science and religion? I think in Dawkins' case it is painfully clear that his atheism colors his view of science for he has written that Darwinism has enabled him to be an intellectually satisfied atheist.

2. Brooke, *Science and Religion*, 5
3. Lennox, *God's Undertaker*, 23.
4. Brooke, *Science and Religion*, 2, 4, 5.
5. Lennox, *God's Undertaker*, 21.

Reasons for Believing that God Exists

Modern physics confirms that the universe has a cause, but early Christian and medieval Islamic philosophy were already making use of the idea of the universe having a cause as a reason to believe in God's existence many centuries ago. The philosopher William Lane Craig's version of the Cosmological Argument can be formulated as follows:

1. If the universe came into existence, it has a cause.

2. The universe came into existence.

Therefore:

3. The universe has a cause.[6]

The crucial proposition in the Kalam Cosmological Argument is two. If the universe has always been there, it did not have a beginning and therefore is uncaused. The belief that the universe has always been there was the prevailing view of the modern scientific era that followed on from Galileo, Copernicus, and Newton. The consensus within contemporary cosmology, however, is that the universe had a beginning and as Arno Penzias, the Nobel Prize winner for physics reminds us, it came out of nothing.[7]

The word nothing is very significant. Something cannot come out of nothing. So, if there was nothing before the universe, and if the universe cannot create itself, and if the universe is the totality of matter that exists, then what caused the universe was not a material substance, but something non-material. It is this non-material cause that can be called God.

The question that now faces us is whether there is anything more that we can know about God other than 'it' caused everything we know to exist. Clearly, God is mind-blowingly powerful

6. Craig, "The Kalam Cosmological Argument." It was Craig who christened the argument the Kalam Cosmological Argument. The word kalam is the Arabic word for medieval philosophy and therefore seems to be an acknowledgement of the Arabic context from which the argument emerged.

7. Lennox, *God's Undertaker*, 58.

otherwise it could not have caused the universe. Is the universe somehow a consequence of something inherent in God? Are there other causes alongside God? Is God an unconscious, non-material cause, or did God 'intend' to create the universe?

In that final question it seems like I am jumping the gun for I am bringing into the picture a personal cause which sounds very much like the God of theism! On Craig's Cosmological Argument alone there is no warrant to go beyond asserting a cause to the universe which is outside of the universe to saying that the God of theism was the cause. There is a huge gap between these two statements, but there is a bridge.

Beginning to close the gap

How might we start to close the gap? One of the ways in which we understand a cause is by looking at what it causes. When we read *The God Delusion*, we can infer reasonably that one of the causes of the book is the writer, Richard Dawkins, who is a person with strong atheist opinions. I say a person because I know from experience that people write books and they are accepted for publication. I know that books do not create other books, therefore Dawkins is not a book himself. Dawkins has also declared his authorship of this book and his claim to authorship has been legally affirmed. On many occasions Dawkins has stated he is an atheist and others can corroborate this. *The God Delusion* like any other book contains the thoughts, feelings, and opinions of the writer. It reveals that Dawkins is a sublimely talented scientist who communicates lucidly his extensive knowledge.

Dawkins alone is not the cause of the book. Others were involved such as the editor, the proofreaders, and the typesetters. There are non-human causes set into motion by humans too such as the chemical reactions that cause ink and glue and the mechanical causes that bind the book together and reproduce it.

Knowing all of this, we can see that there are very important differences talking about the causes of *The God Delusion* and the cause or causes of the universe. The writing of *The God Delusion* is an example of an action that has happened many times, namely the writing of books, whereas the universe's coming into being was a singular act. (We shall see later why the multiverse theory is only speculation.) On the basis of the fact that we know from experience that books are written and produced by people, we can accept that Dawkins is the author of *The God Delusion*. The universe's emergence is an unrepeated act, so I cannot conclude inductively what the cause was. In the creation of *The God Delusion*, pre-existing materials were used such as the chemicals that constitute the ink and glue and the wood that was transformed into paper. Dawkins himself was a pre-existing cause; so too were all the other human beings who collaborated on his book. The universe came out of nothing and its causation brought into being that which had not existed before. Whatever caused the universe is a very different kind of cause in terms of the magnitude of what it causes and because it brought things into existence not from pre-existing materials, but from nothing. Nevertheless, we can look at the universe in order to understand some features of the cause just as we can look at *The God Delusion* and surmise the characteristics of its causes. It is my proposal that a reasonable explanation for the universe is what the philosopher and theologian, Keith Ward, calls the God Hypothesis: A mind that has always existed and always will, and has perceptions, thoughts, and emotions, yet possesses no body.[8] In other words, an unembodied mind of incomprehensible intelligence.

For such a mind to exist, it would first have to be possible for the mind to be independent of brains, for without the universe yet in existence there would be no brains. Of the three ways in which the nature of the mind is understood, two if true would rule out a mind that caused the universe. The first of the two is reductive materialism which is the majority view among contemporary philosophers. Simply put, this is the view that the mind is the brain. Sir Colin Blakemore, Emeritus Oxford Professor of Neuroscience, sums up this view when he declares that the brain is a machine

---

8. Ward, *Why There Almost Certainly Is a God*, 17.

that is the origin of all our actions, beliefs, and thoughts.[9] If re-ductive materialism is true of all minds, the cause of the universe could not have been a mind for without the universe there are no brains as far as we can tell. The other of the two is non-reductive materialism which states that when matter reaches a certain type of high complexity, a mind will emerge. The mind remains depen-dent upon the matter from which it has emerged and dies when the matter dies. Such a mind cannot be the universe's cause as no matter exists before the universe exists. Substance dualism is the view that there are two different substances that account for the mind-brain relationship: the physical brain and the non-physical mind. On this view, it is believed that the mind is independent of and beyond the brain, but that they interact.[10] It is the mind's in-dependence of, but interaction with the brain that opens the door to the God-Hypothesis and to the view that mind can act upon matter. So, what reasons might we have for asserting that minds can exist independently of brains?

The philosopher Frank Jackson's thought experiment about a hypothetical scientist reveals the problem at the heart of reduc-tive materialism. He asks us to consider Mary who is an expert in the science of human sight. She understands everything that science says about the eye and how it is connected to the brain. The interesting thing about Mary is that she is blind. Jackson asks whether Mary would learn something new about human sight if miraculously she received her sight. His answer is yes. No matter how much Mary knows about how human sight works, she has never experienced it for herself. When she receives her sight, she has first-hand experience of what it is like to see. Scientific knowl-edge alone therefore cannot explain personal experience.[11]

Jackson's thought experiment is an example of what the phi-losopher David Chalmers calls the hard problem of consciousness.[12] How do we get from the brain's neuronal functioning, which science

9. Dirckx, *Am I just my brain?*, 19.

10. Ibid., 12.

11. Jackson, "What Mary Didn't Know," 291–95.

12. Dirckx, *Am I just my brain*, 46.

describes, to the lived experience of being who we are? A reductive materialist might argue that one day science and philosophy will close that gap. But why is that response any better than arguing that the gap in our understanding exists because there is indeed a gap between neurons and mind because though they interact, they are not the same?

Reductive materialism and non-reductive materialism are also called into question by some interesting phenomena noted by neuroscience. Neuroscientist, Adrian Owen, has studied for two decades patients with brain trauma. His question has been this: Can a patient in a vegetative state still be conscious? (A vegetative state is one in which the cerebrum, which controls thought and behavior no longer functions, though those parts of the brain which control vital functions such as temperature continue to function.) If either reductive or non-reductive materialism is true, then such a patient will not be conscious. But by using brain-imaging techniques, Owen and his research team came to the startling conclusion that a minority of patients in vegetative conditions can be conscious.[13]

If human minds can exist independently of brains, then it is not an impossibility that a mind could pre-exist the universe from whose matter brains come. If human minds can interact with brains in order to cause bodily states such as psychosomatic illnesses, it is not an impossibility that a mind of immeasurable magnitude and intelligence can cause and shape a universe.

When we look at the universe, we see that it is ordered. If the universe were not ordered, it would be impossible to write this book or for you to read it. Natural science describes this order in terms of uniformity in the behavior of matter. Scientific 'laws' are descriptions of regularities. It is these regularities that enable science to make stunningly accurate predictions such as when solar eclipses will happen. Science's limitation is that it cannot explain why there is order in the universe in the first place, since scientific explanation presupposes order before it can explain anything. The question now is what could cause matter to be ordered? One possible answer is a mind.

13. Owen *et al*, "Detecting Awareness in the Vegetative State," 1402.

We see many examples of minds that create order. For example, inventors construct their inventions, architects design buildings, and town planners plan towns. On a simpler level, we bring order whenever we establish rules of conduct in the home or classroom. A shopping list is the product of a mind seeking to bring order to the mundane yet essential task of shopping. Of course, minds create disorder also through incompetence or mental illness. For a mind to organize the world external to it, it must be ordered itself. If a mind organized the universe, it is itself organized to an unimaginably high level of intelligence.

The Intelligibility of the Universe

If the universe is ordered, it is intelligible scientifically. Has it ever crossed your mind that the fact that scientists can understand the universe is surprising? This is something I know I take for granted and yet Albert Einstein found the comprehensibility of the universe to be the most incomprehensible feature of it. He referred to it as a miracle for it was his opinion that one should expect a chaotic universe which would be incomprehensible.[14]

Humans appear to have an advantage in terms of the earth's position in the universe. Aristotle made the anthropomorphic assumption that the earth was at the heart of the universe. This view has been rejected by modern science. What modern scientists such as Guillermo Gonzalez and Jay W. Richards assert is that the earth occupies a position in the universe which is excellent for understanding it. For example, we live where there is the right amount of starlight to make observations. In fact, according to Gonzalez and Richards, our position allows us to make an impressive range of measurements from cosmology and astronomy to astrophysics and geophysics.[15]

Not only are humans living in an ordered universe and have an excellent vantage point from which to explore it, they also have

14. Lennox, *God's Undertaker*, 60.
15. Ibid., 72

the perfect language with which to describe it-mathematics. The strange thing about mathematics is that it was developed without reference to the universe and then was found to be the best way of describing it. The mathematical physicist, Sir Roger Penrose, makes an eye-catching claim when he opines that mathematics is too good a set of ideas to be a survivor of ideas that have arisen in a random way, as natural selection claims.[16]

Now the universe's intelligibility to humans who can observe it well and who have a language to describe it may be a wonderful cosmic and biological accident. But the idea that it was all an accident is no more convincing than that it was all set up to be understood by us.

The Fine-Tuning Argument

By the fine-tuning argument we mean that the constants of nature are delicately balanced, for if they were either larger or smaller, there could be no life in the universe. The mathematician, John Lennox, gives as examples the carbon atom's energy level and the universe's rate of expansion which if they were very slightly different, no life would have formed.[17] The physicist, Paul Davies, tells us that the stars would not have formed if the ratio of the strong nuclear force to the electromagnetic force had been different by 1 part in 10 to the power of 16.[18] With such extraordinarily improbable precision in operation, the chance that the universe was set up that way seems a plausible hypothesis and no less plausible than that it was the consequence of a gigantically lucky accident.

Opponents of the fine-tuning argument argue that we should not be surprised at fine tuning, for without it we would not be here to be surprised by it in the first place. This is a form of the weak anthropic argument which says that an observable universe will be structured in a way that permits observers to observe it. It is hard

16. Ibid., 61.
17. Ibid., 70.
18. Ibid.

to see what these opponents are really saying other than the obvious: That an observable universe can be observed. Moreover, there is still room to wonder at ourselves for an observable universe is not necessarily also one that is being observed. In other words, the universe might be observable, but the quality of being able to be observed does not mean that there will be human beings in that universe to observe it. This is demonstrated through the philosopher John Leslie's firing squad example. Imagine that Janice is to be executed by firing squad. Fifty sharpshooters are lined up and fire at her. All of them miss. Would we really be able to say to Janice that she ought not to be surprised that she is still alive since unless they had all missed, she would not be alive to be surprised? Janice would be within her rights to ask why they had all missed as it was very unlikely that they would. She would also be within her rights to speculate as to whether they deliberately missed her.[19] The same holds for the universe. It is a necessary condition if the universe is to be observed for it to be conducive to the existence of observers, such as human beings. But we are left with the question: What sufficient reasons came into play to ensure that those necessary conditions, such as the right relationship between the four basic forces, were fulfilled? And what brought about observers such as humans who seem to be such excellent observers as modern physics and astronomy demonstrate and who have developed the language of mathematics to do so?

The multiverse is an attempt to explain the highly unlikely balancing of the universe's constants. If there is a growing plenitude of universes, perhaps an infinitude of universes alongside ours, then eventually one will emerge with the right balances for life. It is like rolling two dice, but obviously much more complicated: If we keep rolling the dice, we will get a double six.

The first problem with the multiverse is that it is an enormous and hypocritical violation of Occam's Razor. As you know, the Razor is the belief that in explaining something, we ought to aim to use as few explanatory factors as possible. The simplest explanation is the preferable one. It is true that by adding divine causation

19. Ibid., 74.

we are adding another type of causation to material causation, but by arguing for the multiverse its proponents are spectacularly multiplying the number of causes. Surely one creator God who has created one universe is more economical than an infinity of universes? Another problem is that the multiverse theory is, as John Polkinghorne, the quantum theorist, states, speculation. In other words, there is no evidence for it and it remains a postulation rather than a fact.[20] The philosopher, Alvin Plantinga, presents a third problem for atheists. The many worlds theory of quantum mechanics envisages that all logically possible worlds exist. As God is logically possible, He exists in at least one of the logically possible worlds. If God is omnipotent, then He can exist in every logically possible world.[21] The multiverse theory therefore is a serious liability for the atheist cause rather than a get-out tactic.

What about Darwin?

Darwinism is atheist science's frontline against religious belief. Framing the debate as one of rational science against superstitious religion, atheists regard evolution as having rendered a divine creator redundant. I personally know of a biology graduate who gave up her Christian faith because of Darwinian evolution. What exactly is this theory? Darwin's theory of evolution is that complex creatures evolve from simpler ancestors over time. Random genetic mutations occur within a creature's genetic code and those mutations that aid survival are preserved. This phenomenon is called natural selection. When the creatures with these survival-enhancing qualities reproduce, they pass them on to their offspring. Therefore, tiger cubs inherit their parents' striped camouflage. Over time more mutations occur. The beneficial ones are preserved, build up, and eventually produce an entirely different creature. The theory of evolution challenges the creation account of Genesis which presents species being created instantly

20. Ibid., 74–75.
21. Ibid., 76.

and remaining unchanged. It provides a mechanism for under-standing the variety of flora and fauna on earth without reference to God's purposes because evolution is an unguided, purposeless process. There have been a range of Christian responses and we will now examine them. It must be admitted that one can hold any of the following views and still be able to describe oneself as a Christian. What will become clear in this section is the inter-pretation I favor.

Liberal theologians have understood the first eleven chapters of Genesis as inspiring narratives rather than accurate science and history.[22] The stories of God's creation, Adam and Eve, and Noah operate like parables rather than as descriptions of what actually happened. The advantage of this point of view is that it avoids the debate over whether these stories are true scientifically and his-torically. The challenge this viewpoint faces is having to explain why myth ends at the end of chapter eleven. It raises the question as to which other parts of Scripture can be classified as myth also.

In the evangelical camp, three ways of understanding creation and evolution have been proposed. First, it is argued that Genesis does not provide answers to how, but why God created the world. Like the liberals, these evangelicals see the Garden of Eden and the story of Adam and Eve as poetic, not literal truths. As Genesis is not a scientific textbook but a spiritual and moral guide, Christians can embrace Darwinism. Theistic evolutionists, as they are called who take this position, believe that God created the universe and then let material processes take their course with human beings showing up eventually.[23] In the theistic evolutionist camp are some extraordinarily able scientists who are also very fine Christians: the biologist, Francis Collins, the biochemist, Michael Behe, and the paleo-biologist, Simon Conway Morris.[24] Collins takes the view that God set up the process of evolution and let it run on its own accord, though intervening at the point that human beings emerge

---

22. Groothuis, *Christian Apologetics*, 269.

23. Ibid., 270.

24. Lennox, *Seven Days*, 162–64.

to confer upon them His image.[25] Behe and Conway Morris, on the other hand, believe that God supervises the evolutionary process to ensure that it produces the organisms that He wants.[26]

If you wish to take the theistic evolution explanation, you are in good company. The explanation that evolution gives for the complexity and changes in species does not exclude God any more than an understanding of how a Ford car works is an argument for the non-existence of Henry Ford, the inventor of the Ford cars.[27] However, theistic evolution faces a specific form of the problem of suffering: Would a morally perfect and absolutely loving God set up the natural selection process to achieve the sorts of creatures He wants through a process of evolution that involves unimaginable amounts of suffering?

Another interpretation is called scientific creationism as pioneered by the Institute for Creation Research. Scientific creationism argues that no more than 10,000 years ago, God created everything in six literal twenty-four hour days.[28]

Those who hold this view are commendably taking Scripture seriously, but in the light of the evidence for the great age of the earth it is important to emphasize that there is another understanding of what Genesis means when it describes God creating over six days. The day-age view understands the days as periods of time of unspecified length.[29] The Early Church fathers Justin Martyr and Irenaeus, long before Darwin posited evolution, suggested that the days represented long sections of time, using Psalm 90:4 as evidence: "For a thousand years in Your sight are like yesterday when it is past, and like a watch in the night."[30] By adopting the view that Genesis uses the word day to refer to long periods of time, we can accommodate the abundant evidence for the earth's great age into a biblical faith. How do scientists know that the earth is very old?

25. Ibid.,163.

26. Ibid.,164.

27. Lennox, *God's Undertaker*, 89.

28. Groothuis, *Christian Apologetics*, 273.

29. Lennox, *Seven Days*, 44.

30. Ibid., 41.

There are three lines of evidence. First, for the earth to be old, the universe would have to be older. Cosmology, which is the study of how the universe is structured, has measured the speed of light and the distance stars are from earth. Cosmologists can therefore measure how long light has taken to get from the stars to earth. Their calculations reveal that the universe is very old. Second, geology is the study of the earth's rocks. It is the consensus among geologists that the formation of the earth's different types of rock required millions of years. Earth's rocks have also been shaped by the weather and the effects of glaciers over a long period of time. Finally, paleontology studies the fossil record. The best interpretation of the fossil record held by all paleontologists is that plants and animals reveal that organisms have lived on earth for millions of years.[31]

Progressive creationism is the third option. I agree with the philosopher, Douglas Groothuis, that this is the best option for it most closely fits both the creation account and scientific knowledge.[32] According to Groothuis, progressive creationism makes six claims:

1. God created the universe *ex nihilo*.

2. God created each kind specially, not through a long, naturalistic process of macroevolution. However, we cannot say with certainty that a biblical kind corresponds to what biologists call a species (although they may be very similar).

3. Species may change and adapt to their environment in various limited ways, given the natures God has given them.

4. A considerable amount of time elapsed between the creation of other species and the creation of humans.

5. God created human beings specially, not through a long process of naturalistic evolution.

6. The first human couple was specially created by God and experienced the Fall in time.[33]

31. Coulter, "Let There Be Light."
32. Groothuis, *Christian Apologetics*, 274.
33. Ibid., 274–75.

Point one is supported by cosmology's view that the universe came out of nothing. Point three agrees with microevolution. Point two conflicts with macroevolution. But there are big problems with the notion of macroevolution.

First, if Darwinism is true, we would expect to see the process operating now in terms of there being organisms that are transitions from one species to another. But we do not see that. Rather than a spectrum of organisms that contains transitional organisms on their way to creating new species, we see a great diversity of species which are distinct from each other.[34]

Gaps in the fossil record pose a serious problem also for macroevolution. Darwin anticipated that transitional forms would be discovered and the gaps in the fossil record would be filled in. He has been proven wrong. As paleontologist, George G. Simpson, concludes: Every paleontologist knows that all types of organism above the level of family are not reached through transitional forms, but appear suddenly in the fossil record. In the Cambrian explosion, for example, a very large number of new species suddenly appeared in a very short period of time which was too short for these species to have evolved over time as Darwinism expects.[35]

The science of genetics did not exist when Darwin postulated his theory of natural selection. In other words, he was ignorant of the way in which offspring inherit their parents' characteristics. But genetics poses some serious problems for Darwinism.[36]

Natural selection proceeds based on random genetic mutations happening, yet organisms seem to be mutation-averse. Mutations are usually harmful. Faulty genes cause diseases and conditions such as cancer and miscarriages. Minor mutations can be tolerated, but major ones cannot. Bodies therefore resist mutation by killing cells whose DNA has mutated and to correct mutations before they are replicated.[37]

---

34. Coulter, "Let There Be Light."

35. Ibid.

36. Ibid.

37. Ibid.

Furthermore, natural selection narrows genetic information rather than diversifying it. Imagine mammal X which hunts in thick jungle, but is itself hunted by a larger predator. There is diversity within species X, but over time natural selection will favor those members of the species which are larger, better camouflaged, have excellent hearing, and sense of smell. After a certain period, there will be left no members of species X below a certain size, level of camouflage, and capacity to hear and smell. The genes for those animals below this survival threshold will have been eliminated from the gene pool. Natural selection therefore does not lead to new genetic information.[38]

What about point five which presents humanity as God's special creation and not a product of a long evolutionary process? Surely this is refuted by the evidence of precursors of modern humans? The geneticist, Paul Coulter, argues that the way bones which seem to have human properties are interpreted depends upon the prior convictions of those interpreting them. Those who conclude that humans are the result of natural selection will reconstruct whole skeletons based upon discoveries of small amounts of bone in ways that they think the common ancestor of humans and other primates would have looked like. These bones can also be interpreted as extinct species of primates or the bones of humans with deformities and disabilities. It was once conceived that Neanderthals were evolutionary ancestors of modern humans, but now it is believed that they were a distinct species or a subgroup within the human population.[39]

The Bible presents the idea that humans are special because they are made in the image of God (Gen. 1:27). What does this deeply mysterious and exciting statement mean? Peter May, a retired medical doctor who writes on Christian apologetics, has provided some valuable insights into its meaning.[40] May's hypothesis consists of three propositions:

38. Ibid.
39. Ibid.
40. May, "What is the Image of God"?

1. That being made in the image of God is what distinguishes humans from the rest of creation.

2. That understanding who God is through what he has revealed about himself will teach us what it means to be made in his image.

3. That there are six human features that constitute our image-likeness to God.

I will present a summary of May's argument below.

Humans are creative

Animals are creative in a very limited way. For example, birds create nests, but they do so according to an instinctive pattern that leads to the creation of the same type of nest each year. Birds are not observed improving the design or experimenting with new nest structures.

God is creative to a degree beyond human understanding. He is the author of the whole universe. One could add to May's argument the biblical teaching that God will create a new heaven and a new earth (Rev. 21:2). When a person becomes a Christian, s/he becomes a new creation in terms of their behavior (2 Cor. 5:17). God is the author of this profound change. God rested after His first series of creative acts as described in Genesis 1 and 2, but he will create new worlds in the future and is busy initiating creative change in His children.

Though limited in their creativity in comparison to God, humans possess genuine creativity. May gives the personal example of his uncle who designed the power plants for North Sea oil rigs. He also refers to the ubiquity of inventions across human cultures. We can add to May's argument examples of how humans are creative in terms of aesthetics. Composers, writers, and painters are good examples. It is important to recognize that all individual humans are creative to varying degrees, A person may not be a creative genius like Edison or Picasso, but his or her creativity may shine through the coordination of the colors s/he wears, or the way s/he decorates his or her house.

Humans are intelligent

May argues that creation reflects the mind of the creator. Creation required immense intelligence on the part of the creator. Human intelligence is not on God's scale, but it is superior to anything found among the animals. One distinctive feature of our intelligence is our capacity to ponder why we exist at all, something that animals take for granted. May makes the very relevant point that obscurantist Christianity and evangelism that deny the importance of apologetics fail to recognize human beings' minds and therefore the totality of their humanity.

Humans have an aesthetic sense

Humans can appreciate beauty. May refers to his ownership of a place by the seaside. From that spot he can see over Christchurch Bay and out towards the Isle of Wight and the Needles, which are large, tall rocks sticking up out of the sea. Whilst sitting there, May observes people who are taking in the view and are overawed by its beauty. He notes that often these people are walking dogs. But unlike their owners, the dogs do not even notice the view.

Humans are moral

May describes how animals do not feel guilt and do not think in terms of good and evil. Humans are moral beings who reflect the nature of God who is the definitive moral being. I would add that though humans often do wrong things, the great majority know they have done wrong and all can think in terms of right and wrong, even if their moral sense is warped. Moreover, there has been remarkable agreement across human cultures over time and space as to what is right and wrong.

Humans are relational

To prove his point, May points to novels and soap operas which demonstrate that the most important matter of human existence is relationships, and in particular, love. I would add that films and stage plays demonstrate this too. As further evidence, May points to the collapse of meaningful relationships as the biggest cause of suicide. The most relational person is God who calls all humans to a relationship with him which is the most fulfilling relationship on offer.

Humans are spiritual

May's evidence for this statement is that until the twentieth century every culture has had at its heart belief in a god or gods. Even though atheist communist regimes tried to suppress religious belief in the twentieth century, with their collapse came a revival of religious belief. In our supposedly post-religious Western world, New Age beliefs to some extent have replaced organized religious practice. I would add that throughout the rest of the world, humanity remains overwhelmingly religious.

May's conclusion

May concludes that an image of something reflects the original. Regardless of how good a reflection that image is, there is a constant reality behind that image. This reality has been made known to us through the incarnation of God in human form as Jesus Christ (John 1:18).

The Need for Human Humility

There is indeed something very special and unique about humans. I say this not because I am human, but because of the reasons May gives. However, I am sure May would agree with me that though humans are at the pinnacle of creation, this does not mean that we can lord it over the rest of creation. We must remember that creation does not belong to us. It is God's and we are to treat it with respect. It is a defining feature of being a good human that we have empathy for species other than our own. Thus, as far as I am aware, no carnivorous animal has chosen to be a vegetarian or vegan.

Evolution can explain the form life takes, but not the fact that it exists in the first place.

As the medical doctor and scientist, Stuart Kauffman, asserts: It is foolish to claim to know how life started on Earth because no one knows.[41] Michael Behe, the biochemist, has demonstrated the problem through his concept of irreducible complexity which says that certain natural structures cannot function unless all their parts are there and ready to work. Behe uses the metaphor of a mouse trap to illustrate his point. A mouse trap cannot trap mice unless it has a hammer to do the trapping, a bar to hold the hammer down, a spring to close the hammer very quickly, and a base on which all these parts can be mounted. Unless all these parts are present the mouse trap is useless. In terms of biological structures, Behe gives the example of the single cell. For the cell to function, all its very complex parts must be in place at the same time. They cannot emerge over time into a fully functioning cell as evolutionary development says they will. All the parts must be there at the start otherwise the cell cannot function.[42]

In the Beginning was the Word

It is significant that Genesis 1:11, 12 describe God speaking or commanding creation into existence. For example:

> 'Then he commanded, "Let the earth produce all kinds of plants, those that bear grain and those that bear

41. Lennox, *God's Undertaker*, 122.
42. Coulter, "Let There Be Light."

fruit"—and it was done. So the earth produced all kinds of plants, and God was pleased with what he saw.'

In response to divine language, the world came forth. This sounds like metaphor rather than realism, but there is a language that is the basis of the forms that biological life takes. Deoxyribonucleic acid, or DNA as it is popularly known, exists in every cell of an organism's body. Most DNA lies in the cells' nuclei and is known as nuclear DNA. The information in DNA is a code that consists of four chemical bases: adenine (A), guanine (G), cytosine (C), and thymine (T). The order in which these bases appear determines how an organism is constructed and maintained.

The problem that DNA poses to those who argue that unguided, mindless, natural forces produced life is explaining the origin of DNA's complicated information. As geophycisist Stephen Meyer explains, DNA resembles human and computer languages. As such languages are produced by intelligences, it is not unreasonable to suggest that DNA is the product of an intelligence also.[43]

The skeptic might argue that we are employing the God-of-the gaps argument. We cannot see how a language like DNA could emerge as a product of unthinking, natural forces, so we say God did it. But this is not a God-of-the-gaps argument. It is rather an abductive argument: An inference to the best explanation warranted by the information we have rather than a postulation filling in for our ignorance.

Morality Hints at God's Existence

Naturalism boils down to the view that all that there is, is matter. Moral values, on this view therefore, are only pieces of matter. So why is one piece of matter morally true and another morally false?

We are told by materialists that humans are an evolved species that has during its past evolved morality in order to survive in groups which offer the best chance of survival. Hence, we cooperate, keep our promises, and act altruistically. But moral thinking

---

43. Meyer, "DNA and Other Things."

seems to be concerned with far more than personal or group survival. Self-sacrifice has been and is often seen as a good moral thing. Those who sacrifice themselves in battle for the good of others are awarded Victoria Crosses and Purple Hearts.

But evolution, if true, has also encoded within us very nasty adaptations such as xenophobia and the capacity for genocide. How do we judge what is right in our evolutionary heritage? To do so, we need to think outside of our evolutionary inheritance. But does this not make humans special? Does this not bring us closer to the notion that we are made in the image of God who also stands outside of evolution?

3

Does God Have Anything to Do With Us?

SCIENTIFIC DISCOVERY AND MORALITY may point to God, but that does not solve the question as to whether Jesus rose from the dead because of that God. As the apostle Paul wrote to the Corinthians, without the Resurrection there is no Christianity. But if Jesus was not God the Son in human form, and he was raised for some reason by a super angel acting independently of an indifferent, deistic type God, or in the absence of any God, there can be no Christianity either. Is there evidence that Jesus was God the Son and that God the Father raised him? Answering that question not only solves the problem of who raised Jesus, but also gives us an understanding of what God is like.

Christianity says yes, Jesus is God the Son and that God the Father raised him because of his love for him. To understand why we ought to believe this, we must first begin by asking whether Jesus claimed to be God in the first place. If he did not, it is not clear why we ought to consider him so in the first place.

It is clear from the Gospels that Jesus declared himself to be divine. An interesting summary of all the occasions on which Jesus declared himself to be God and a man can be found in an online article by the Josh MacDowell Ministry.[1] For illustration's sake I shall pick three examples. In John 8:58, Jesus called Himself "I Am", or the eternal and self-sufficient God and came close to being stoned for saying this. The word for God *Theos* is usually reserved as a word for God the Father, but *Theos* is used to describe

1. Josh McDowell Ministry, "Did Jesus really claim to be God?"

Jesus in John's Gospel (1:1, 1:18 and 20:28). Luke 22:70 records that when asked directly by the Sanhedrin whether He was the Son of God, Jesus said yes.

Does the Bible teach that Jesus, who is God the Son in human form, had a father who is God the Father? The answer is yes. You cannot read the Gospels without seeing the multitudinous examples of this. Again, I shall present three examples. In John 5:20, Jesus declared that he did the will of his Father. In his last conversation with his disciples recorded by John, Jesus comforted his disciples by telling them that he was going to his Father's House to prepare a place for them (John 14:1–3). At the moment of his death, Jesus cried, "'Father! In your hands I place my spirit!'" (Luke 23:46).

The skeptic might argue that the Gospels cannot be assumed to be reliable as there are questions over whether the original Gospels, which no longer exist, are historically reliable and that the copies we have today have copying errors within them. Such a skeptic does not realize that many of the twelve facts presented at the start of this book are found in the Gospels. Of the five facts upon which almost all scholars of all persuasions agree, the first three are supported by the Gospels. On that basis already we can say that the Gospels present truthfully three key facts about Jesus' life: That he was born, that he died by crucifixion, and that he was buried. But we need more than that, however, to assert that Jesus claimed to be God the Son and that his Father was God the Father.

Just as Habermas has provided the most robust defense of the Resurrection, so he presents a first class defense of the historical reliability of the Gospels in his online article, 'Recent Perspectives on the Reliability of the Gospels.'[2] It is well worth reading the whole article, but in the space permitted me, I shall select certain points that Habermas makes about how traditionally the New Testament, and therefore the Gospels, have been defended.

To demonstrate that the texts we have today are a result of a trustworthy copying and handing-down process over many centuries, Habermas begins by pointing out that the manuscript

---

2. Habermas, "Recent Perspectives on the Reliability of the Gospels."

evidence for the New Testament is markedly greater than for any other ancient Greek and Roman source. There are more than 5500 copies and part copies of the New Testament, mainly in Greek, but also in other languages. Most classical texts are supported by fewer than ten each. What is most important is that there is very little variation of importance between these copies. Habermas reminds us that having many copies of a document with little variation of note among them is no guarantee that originals were historically accurate. We may have many consistent copies over time of historically inaccurate originals. So how might we assert the historical accuracy of the originals?

Habermas draws our attention to the fact that the New Testament copies are closer to the original writings than any other classical text. They date to a mere one hundred to 150 years after New Testament was completed whereas classical copies date from 700 to 1400 words after their original texts. This means also that the New Testament copies are closer to the actual events they narrate and therefore the writers of the New Testament were in a better position to know truly what had happened. If classical scholars are content to use copies far removed from the originals and the events the originals described, why cannot Christian scholars use the New Testament?

Other traditional means of defending the New Testament consist in showing that the people who were reckoned to have written it actually did write it. This is an area where recent research supports some conservative readings. The arguments that Paul was the writer of the major epistles that bear his name is an example.

With specific reference to the Gospels, Habermas argues that around eighteen non-Christian sources external to the Scriptures confirm many of the details of Jesus' life found in the Gospels. Moreover, early Christian writers like Polycarp confirm those details and they were writing within ten years of the New Testament's completion.

Traditional conservative arguments have provided a general framework with which to understand the New Testament copies as true to their originals and historically reliable. Among more recent scholarship, there is good evidence that the Gospel accounts of Jesus' claim to be divine are historically true. Using the principle of dissimilarity or discontinuity, scholars have concluded that Jesus did indeed use the title Son of Man of himself. The principle of dissimilarity states that a saying can be attributed to someone only if that saying cannot be attributed to other contemporary sources. In the case of Jesus, if one of his purported sayings cannot be attributed to Jewish thinking or the Early Church, then it was something he said. Admittedly, Jewish thinking did have the concept of the Son of Man, but it was never applied to Jesus and none of the New Testament epistles addresses Jesus as the Son of Man.

But is the Son of Man a divine title, as it sounds as if Jesus, by using it, was accentuating his human nature? The answer is that Jesus regarded the Son of Man as synonymous with the Son of God and the Messiah: They are one and the same person. The best evidence in the Gospels for this is found in Matthew 26:62–64:

> 'The High Priest stood up and said to Jesus, "Have you no answer to give to this accusation against you?" But Jesus kept quiet. Again, the High Priest spoke to him, "In the name of the living God I now put you under oath: tell us if you are the Messiah, the Son of God." Jesus answered him, "So you say. But I tell all of you: from this time on you will see the Son of Man sitting at the right side of the Almighty and coming on the clouds of heaven!"'

We can see from the High Priest's question and Jesus' response that the Son of Man was also the Son of God and the Messiah, for when Jesus claimed to be the Son of Man, the High Priest took him to be answering in the affirmative that he was also the Messiah and the Son of God.[3] Therefore, the conclusion of skeptical scholars is that Jesus claimed he was divine. As we shall see, Jesus' claim that he was divine sets up a trilemma that leads to the conclusion that Jesus was indeed divine.

3. Licona, "Jesus—The Son of Man?"

The Trilemma

It may be the case that Jesus claimed to be divine and have a Father, but there is from the skeptics' point of view no reason to accept that this was true. We must go another step further in convincing the skeptic and to do so, we can call upon what is known as the Trilemma which was first presented by the mid-nineteenth century Scottish preacher, John Duncan. For a man to claim that he was divine and that he had a Father in heaven, as Jesus did, he would be one of three things: a liar, a lunatic, or divine.[4] The problem for the skeptic is that if we look at Jesus' moral standards and his logical mind when debating the Pharisees, it is unlikely he was bad or mad. He was therefore what he said he was: God the Son. To escape the Trilemma, Dawkins suggests that Jesus was mistaken. But to say that Jesus mistakenly asserted he was divine is to present Jesus as a monumental fool, and this cannot be asserted in the light of the lucidity and imaginativeness of his teachings.

Miracles

A skeptic has yet another card to play: the arguments against miracles. The Resurrection was a miracle, but if miracles are so unlikely to happen that we might as well not accept that Jesus came back from the dead, then no matter how likely it looks from the historical evidence, Jesus is dead.

Before we consider the arguments against miracles, we need to define what a miracle is. I will use the following definition: A miracle is an event that is an exception to recognized natural or scientific laws.

The argument against the Resurrection has been sustained by the skepticism of the Scottish philosopher and historian David Hume. Hume produced two arguments against miracles. The first is called the argument from the uniformity of nature:

1. Miracles violate nature's laws.

4. Barton, "The History of the Liar, Lunatic, Lord Trilemma."

2. The laws are inviolable.

3. The argument against miracles is as strong as it can be.

The second is called the argument from the uniformity of experience:

1. Unusual, yet frequently observed events are not miracles.

2. A resurrection is a miracle because at no time and place has it been observed.

3. Uniform experience contradicts all miracle claims otherwise they would not be miraculous claims.[5]

Arguments for Miracles: The Problem of Induction

Hume's Argument from the Uniformity of Nature is defeated by his own Problem of Induction. Hume asserts that though it has always been observed that the sun has risen, there is no guarantee that tomorrow it will rise. If we apply his way of thinking to the Resurrection, we find this: Though it has never been the case that anyone has observed a resurrection, there is no guarantee that to-morrow someone will not rise from the grave.[6]

Hume's Circular Argument from the Uniformity of Experience

A circular argument is a fallacy where the arguer begins with what s/he wishes to prove. In other words, the conclusion is one of the premises or assumptions behind one of the premises of an argument. Hume declares that experience is uniform and on that basis discounts the Resurrection. But to say that experience is uniform in the first place, Hume must assume that no resurrections, or any

5. Lennox, *God's Undertaker*, 194–95.
6. Ibid., 195–96.

other kinds of miracles, have taken place. Hume therefore assumes his conclusion at the start of his argument.[7]

Hume's Uncheckable Argument from the Uniformity of Experience

For Hume to be able to say that there has never been a miracle, he would have to check every event in the universe past and present, and that is impossible.[8]

Another Argument against Miracles

This is another one of Hume's arguments and it is one which I was confronted with by two former students of mine. It runs like this: As the disciples lived in a primitive, pre-scientific age, they were prone to believe in superstitious nonsense such as Jesus' resurrection.

This line of reasoning demonstrates remarkable ignorance and arrogance. First, it cannot account for why the highly intellectual and skeptical hater of Christianity, Paul, converted. Second, it fails to recognize that the first reactions of the disciples to Jesus' Resurrection was disbelief. The female disciples who went to the tomb on Sunday morning were perplexed at not finding Jesus' body (Luke 24:1–4; John 20:1–2, 15). The male disciples met the female disciples' news that Jesus had risen with incredulity (Mark 16:11; Luke 24:11). A low level of education does not equate to a low level of skeptical intelligence. One of the most skeptical people I have met outside of academia is the cleaner who cleans my classroom. She was illiterate until a few years ago when she learned to read, yet she possesses a healthy habit of disbelief until she sees good evidence.

---

7. Ibid., 202.
8. Ibid.

Problems with Naturalism

The denial of the possibility of miracles is premised on a naturalistic worldview which argues that the world is only made of matter and there are no gods. Naturalism, however, is a flawed worldview:

1. Naturalism argues that all there is are unconscious material forces acting by chance within a closed system. In a universe of unconscious material, where does consciousness come from?

2. If our minds, or brains, are the products of random, unguided processes, why should we trust them to know the truth, which is neither random nor unstructured? And if we cannot trust them to know the truth, how can we say anything is true, including naturalism?

The Problem of Evil and Pain

Another line of defense for the skeptic is the very tricky problem of evil and pain. If God is so loving and so powerful in that he raised his Son, Jesus, from the dead, why does he permit evil and pain? The arguments from evil and pain are used to disprove the existence of God or argue that God's existence is highly unlikely.

Formally, as an argument it takes two forms: the logical and the evidential. The logical argument runs like this:

1. An all-powerful, all-benevolent, and all-knowing God would not allow evil and pain.

2. Evil and pain exist.

3. Therefore, an all-powerful, all-benevolent, and all-knowing God does not exist.

The evidential argument presents the highly improbable existence of God:

1. An all-powerful, all-benevolent, and all-knowing God would allow evil and suffering.

2. Evil and suffering exist.

3. Therefore, an all-powerful, all good, and all-knowing God most probably does not exist.

The evidential argument leaves open the possibility that there might be no incompatibility between God's existence and the presence of evil and pain.

You may have noticed that I have used two words to describe what is wrong with our world: evil and pain. The problem of evil refers to the problem of human maleficence such as theft, fraud, and murder. The problem of pain refers to the suffering caused by the natural world such as snake bites, epidemics, and earthquakes.

I will not be able to do complete justice to the problems of evil and suffering in the short space that I have, but I will suggest several things that you can say to a skeptic that will take out some of the sting of his or her objection. On the problem of evil, I shall present ideas taken from philosopher William Lane Craig's very fine essay "The Problem of Evil."[9] On the problem of suffering, I shall present neuroscientist and apologist Sharon Dirckx's responses.[10]

With regards to the logical problem of evil, Craig points to his fellow philosopher Alvin Plantinga who argues that the proponent of this argument shoulders a very large burden of proof which s/he cannot bear. There is no necessary contradiction between propositions one and two. If the proponent thinks they are contradictory, s/he must be assuming certain things which are called hidden premises by logicians. Plantinga identifies two: That if God is all-powerful, he can create any world he wants and if he is all good, he will prefer to create a world without evil. If we take the first premise, the atheist is thinking as follows: If God can create any world he wishes, he can therefore create a world in which humans freely only ever choose the morally right thing. If we take the second premise, the atheist has concluded this: If God is all good, He would wish to create a world where humans only ever freely choose to do the morally right thing rather than a world with evil.

9. Craig, "The Problem of Evil."

10. Dirckx, *Why? Looking at God, evil & suffering.*

Plantinga's response is known as the Free Will Defense. Plantinga challenges the hidden premise that an all-powerful God can do everything. Plantinga says he cannot. For instance, God cannot create a square circle, or a round triangle. God therefore cannot create a world in which people have genuine free-will and yet only will perform good actions, for if God creates the conditions in which people only perform good actions, he is causing them to make a particular choice which means they are not genuinely free. God therefore cannot guarantee the outcome of people's decision. Therefore, there is a world which God cannot create, which is a world in which people only freely do what is good.

But what about the second hidden premise: That if God is all-good, he would prefer a world devoid of evil to one that has any amount of evil in it, particularly our world which has a lot. Indeed, atheists and skeptics will sharpen their argument by asking why God permits such a huge amount of evil?

Aware that all he must do to defeat the logical argument from evil is to give a possible reason for why God is compatible with evil, Plantinga provides two:

1. God has a morally sufficient reason to permit evil.

2. God could not have created our world with all its good with less evil.

These two reasons are possible, therefore the logical argument from evil fails. The burden of proof is now on the atheist to demonstrate that there are no possible worlds in which God is all-powerful, all-good, and all-knowing and evil exists.

According to Craig, philosophers have accepted that the logical problem of evil has been solved. The new assault on God comes from the probabilistic argument: On the basis of evil's existence, it is unlikely that God exists.

Craig makes four points in response:

1. Though the existence of evil in the magnitude and quality that it possesses renders God's existence unlikely, the full range of evidence for God's existence actually makes God's

existence probable. Craig lists the following lines of argument and evidences as making God's existence probable: the cosmological argument, the teleological argument, the existence of moral absolutes, the ontological argument for a maximally great being, as well as evidence for the historical fact of the Resurrection. Craig develops his point by arguing successfully that it is possible to believe two propositions, even though one is improbable with respect to the other. He gives as an example our individual existences. Biological reproduction exists, but from the standpoint of biological reproduction, our existence, though a fact, is improbable. If one of X's ancestors in the very long chain of ancestors we each possess had not met and reproduced with another of X's ancestors, X would not exist. We accept the scientific truths of biological reproduction and yet we accept the fact of our own existence. Therefore, though evil makes God seem improbable, it is not impossible to believe that both evil and God exist.

2. Craig employs secondly the argument from our limited minds. As our thoughts and understanding are circumscribed, we are not in a position to judge whether God has or has not probably got good reasons for permitting evil. What seems evil from our perspective might be absolutely good and perfectly justifiable from God's view. Craig denies this is an argument from mystery, but is rather a recognition of our limited thoughts.

3. God may therefore have a morally sufficient reason to permit evil.

4. It is Craig's view that Christian doctrines increase the probability of God and evil existing simultaneously. First, the end of life is not happiness but the knowledge of God. Innocent suffering teaches us to depend more deeply than usual on God. Second, humans and demonic powers are in rebellion against God. It is no surprise therefore if the world is full of evil. Thirdly, suffering can be borne because we have an eternal perspective. All suffering, which is temporary, will be

replaced with perfect joy when God's Kingdom fully arrives on earth. Our suffering will forever be recompensed (2 Cor. 4:16–18). Finally, knowing God is a source of infinite goodness. Regardless of how much we suffer, knowing God is a far greater good.

We might also press the following points. If a skeptic argues that if God exists, he ought not to have created him or her to live in this world of pain and suffering, we can point out that many, many people choose to have children despite the awful suffering that can be experienced. If the skeptic asks why, if God exists, he would tolerate human evil, we can ask why, as God exists, does he tolerate the skeptic's evil. The problem of evil is always discussed with reference to other's evil and never one's personal evil. If a skeptic realizes that one of our beliefs is that God tolerates a person's evil (though there is a limit to this as the Day of Judgement shows) with the aim of bringing that person to a saving knowledge of Him, s/he might be less judgmental of our beliefs about God and evil.

The Problem of Pain

The problem of pain seems to pose a more serious problem to Christians. Moral evil may be the consequence of human free will, but what about epidemics and tsunamis that flood cities? These are independent of human choices and cause great suffering. Why would God allow these to add greatly to the misery already caused by human wickedness? Before we explore some lines of response to this question, let us look at what atheism has to offer as an answer to this question.

Dawkins is well-known for saying that as we live in a universe that has no purpose, but just is the way it is, then our being in such a universe means that there will be suffering for the universe cannot care for human well-being.[11] Epidemics happen because viruses and bacteria that are hostile to human health have evolved. Tsunamis happen because that is the nature of a planet

11. Dawkins, *River Out of Eden*, 133.

that has moving tectonic plates beneath the oceans. That is how it is and humans who are killed by these phenomena are suffering because of living in a world that has not been designed with them in mind, but just is.

But many people appear to have a sense that this is not how things ought to be. Philosophers tell us we cannot derive an ought from an is, but in matters of natural disaster, that is how we often think. Take for example a ship that is caught suddenly in an unforeseen typhoon and sinks within twenty minutes. Every person on board drowns. Our first response is not likely to be that this is simply a consequence of living on a planet with unpredictable typhoons. Our response most likely will be that this ought not to have happened. We might go on to ask how such calamities might be prevented in the future. Perhaps better weather detection equipment is possible. We are not satisfied with how things naturally are. So, where does this dissatisfaction come from?

Dawkins' answer could be that it is part of our religious upbringing. We have been conditioned to think that we are the pinnacle of God's creation, so how dare the world not be the way we want it to be. There is another possibility, however. What if it is the case that the natural world is indeed not how it was intended to be and that our sense of it being other than it should be is a consequence of that?

That is the view of Christianity. When God created the world, he described it as good (Gen. 1:31). It was not intended to be a place of suffering. He created human beings to supervise his creation which can be understood to mean that humans had the task of bringing out the best in what God had made. This, however, raises the question as to why the world has ceased to be a place of enjoyment and fulfilment and has become a world where good things still exist abundantly, but where natural evil is abundant too?

Dirckx provides several very useful responses to this question.[12] One of her responses is to argue that the natural world is broken. On this argument, human sin introduced natural disasters into God's creation. Romans 8:20–22 describes creation as

12. Dirckx, *Why?*, 12–40.

imprisoned in a state of corruption. The good news is that God will one day deliver creation.

One way of understanding the connection between sin and natural disasters is to take into account human responsibility and free will. It is the Jewish and Christian belief that God made humans to be supervisors of His creation (Gen. 1:26, 28). If human beings are truly morally free, God cannot make them choose one way or the other. Human beings for the most part have chosen to manage the Earth independently of God. They make mistakes and act immorally by exploiting the natural world. As a result, some natural disasters have at their root human activity. Some scientists believe that the rise in disasters associated with water is due to a combination of natural and human-made causes. Global warming has increased the temperature of the oceans and the incidence of hurricanes is increasing.[13]

Someone might object by saying that there are indeed natural disasters that have a human cause, but what of those natural disasters that have no human cause? How could an earthquake, which is the result of the movement of tectonic plates against one another, be linked to human sin? Dirckx argues that humans have become disconnected from the natural world. Before yielding to temptation, Adam and Eve lived in harmony with God and with the natural world (Gen. 2:19–20). Once this connection with God and the natural world was severed by sin, humans lost their sensitive awareness of the natural world's signs of events that unless understood, can become natural disasters. Dirckx gives as an example the way cattle seek higher ground before a tsunami hits. They appear to have some sort of sensory mechanism that enables them to predict this sort of danger.[14]

I should like to add another observation that might shed a little light on this tragic mystery. In Genesis 2:7, it is recorded that God made humanity from 'some soil from the ground'. It is also recorded that after Adam sinned, one of the consequences was that the ground was cursed (3:17). Now, Adam would have to work

13. Than, "Humans add to natural disaster risk."
14. Dirckx, Why?, 137.

very hard to grow crops and would have to contend with 'weeds and thorns' (v. 18). He became vulnerable to famine, one of the worst of natural and human-made disasters. Humans would die and 'become soil again' for out of it humans came (v. 19). Animals and birds too were formed out of the ground (2:19). We might hypothesize that when Adam sinned, because he had a supervisory and organic connection to the rest of creation, his disobedience was reproduced within the natural order as chaos and death. As Adam had chosen to disobey God and now was separated from Him, this was and is paralleled in a created sphere troubled to its core by the presence of sin.

But as we have noted earlier when discussing Darwinism and the survival of the fittest, on the Christian view natural suffering will come to an end. The natural order will be healed by God of its corruption and restored to what he intended it to be (Rom. 8:20–21). The atheist worldview has the universe's heat death as its end game.

A Conclusion Thus Far

We have covered a lot of ground and so it is appropriate to stop and take stock of what we have concluded so far.

We have seen that the best explanation for what happened after Jesus died was that he rose from the dead. It is possible that Jesus was not raised from the dead by God, but by a super-angel with death-solving powers. To refute this notion, we have explored how science and morality signpost the existence of God and how the Gospel texts and the Trilemma provide good grounds for believing that God the Son came into our world in the form of Jesus and that God the Father raised him from the dead. We have also explored some responses to the logical and evidential problems of evil and the problem of suffering.

Let us now proceed to examine certain popular objections that the skeptic might throw our way.

Other Serious Matters

Who Made God?

THIS IS A QUESTION that children are known to ask. That does not mean it is a childish question as it concerns the nature of God's being. It can be a challenging question because it is used by skeptics in response to the assertion that God is a reasonable explanation for the universe. If the Christian cannot answer the question, the skeptic seems justified in rejecting God as an explanation.

I do not think it is by any means a decisive objection. First, not being able to explain the origin of X does not cast doubt on X's existence. Ancient people may not have known the origin of thunder and lightning, but none of them doubted its existence.

The question of who made God is troubling to the Christian because it implies that there is someone who is greater than God. A hyper-god, or a mega-god if you like. Christianity, however, teaches that God is the highest or maximal being. How then do we respond to this question?

Ward answers the question as follows. He says that as we can think of things existing in time, like chairs, people, and horses, we can conceive of things existing outside of time, though we may not be able to name them. What exists outside of time is time-less or eternal. It has always been there and therefore does not have a cause. Yet, that eternal thing could cause things to exist in time. Christians call that eternal thing God who is therefore an uncaused Creator. The question who made God is therefore meaningless.[1] It is what philosophers call a category mistake because it is categorizing God as a caused being when He is un-caused by definition.

God's Judgement is Too Harsh

Would God really condemn people who though not perfect have done more good than bad? The problem with this view is that it fails to see that as the Bible declares: "everyone has sinned and is far away from God's saving presence" (Rom. 3:23). Like a human judge, a morally perfect God must punish wrongdoing because He is just. The goodness of people does not prevent their being punished if they do something wrong. A driver might obey all the red lights on his journey, but let us imagine that at the final junction of his journey he decides to jump the red light because he has realized he is running late. A traffic officer sees him do this and pulls him over and issues a fine. It is no good the driver arguing that on all the other occasions he obeyed the lights. The fact that on this occasion he did not requires punishment because it could have led to the death of the driver and other motorists.

God's standard is the complete and perfect keeping of His law. Why would God compromise on anything less than the complete keeping of a perfect moral standard? If we know we ought to be good, we know we should be wholly good all the time, even though we know we cannot attain that standard.

It is important that we do not allow the conversation to stop at this point. Someone who is troubled by God's seemingly harsh, judgmental nature needs to know that God's judgement is a consequence of his love and that his love for us has provided a glorious means to salvation.

The story of Jonah provides a way of understanding God as one who judges evil because of his love and yet because of his love, he provides a way of escape from his judgement. Jonah, an Old Testament prophet, was sent to Nineveh, the capital city of the

---

1. Ward, *Why There Almost Certainly Is a God*, 52–53.

Assyrian Empire, to declare that God was going to punish the Nin-evites for their wickedness (Jon. 1:1, 2). By warning the Ninevites of their impending judgement, God was giving them time to change their ways. Jonah refused to obey God, perhaps because he feared going to a city with such an appalling reputation and perhaps be-cause he did not think that the Ninevites deserved the chance to repent. When Jonah fled from God by taking a boat to Tarshish, God pressurized Jonah into going to Nineveh by causing him to be swallowed up by a specially prepared sea creature (1:17). Jonah's mission was too important for him to be allowed to refuse it.

We can see what sin had incurred God's judgement for in response to Jonah's warning, the king and nobles of Nineveh is-sued a decree in which they commanded everyone to repent of their evil ways (3:8). God's judgement had been provoked because violence hurts people and ends their lives. It is his love for people that causes God to intervene on behalf of victims. But as God loves all people, both the victims and the violent, he provides the violent with time to repent. On this occasion, the violent repented and turned from their ways and God relented (3:10).

The same warning applies to all people. We may not be violent, but all have sinned and stand under God's judgement, for as Jesus taught, all manner of sins come out of the heart of people (Matt. 15:19–20). Yet, as possibly the most famous verse of Scripture tells us, there is a glorious escape route: "For God loved the world so much that He gave His only Son, that everyone who believes in Him may not die but have eternal life" (John 3:16). Rather than suffering the penalty for our sins, Jesus took it for us. We can either accept this gift of salvation or reject it. If we accept it, God becomes our Father. If we reject it, we will pay the penalty for our evil.

The Question of Hell

Some people might concede that God must keep order in His world and so punishment is needed. But, one of the problems people have with Christianity is the idea of hell. It is the prospect of everlasting punishment that seems excessive and sadistic. Why should people suffer forever and irrevocably for the wrong, finite things they have done? It seems like a massive overreaction on God's part. What can we say to unbelievers about this phenomenon?

Our first response could be that there are a range of views of hell in Christianity. The two most common are the view of everlasting, conscious torment (ECT), which is the most common, and the minority, conditional immortality/annihilationist view which believes that humans are not immortal unless they are born again, and therefore when the unredeemed, who are not born again, are judged by God, they are annihilated. The second might seem more merciful, but it depends on whether one thinks non-existence is a more brutal punishment than ECT or whether ECT is so horrifying, it is better not to exist. As ECT is the most common understanding of hell, it is the defense of that viewpoint that we will now explore.

Hell cannot be discussed without the context of God's mercy and grace. It is important to emphasize that God has done everything he can to help people avoid his judgement without overriding their free-will. What more could God the Father do than what he has already done: To send his Son in human form to die the worst kind of death the ancient world had devised and experience the full force of divine wrath as a substitute for sin? God endures the horrors of human sin because of his "great kindness, tolerance, and patience." It is his goodness that leads us to repentance (Rom. 2:4). God has also left people the testimony of his Bible, of his body (which is the Church of true believers), and of the glory of his creation.

Thus, God does not want anyone to perish, but all to receive eternal life (John 3:16- 17). He is not the tyrannical God of Hitchens and Dawkins' imaginations, rubbing his anthropomorphic hands at the sight of sinners plunging headfirst into the eternal bonfire. We see this in Jesus' lamentations over Jerusalem because it refused his offer of forgiveness (Matt. 23:37). As he suffered on the cross, Jesus asked his Father to forgive those who had crucified him because they were ignorant of what they were doing (Luke 23:34). God is clearly a lot more merciful than people who are content to tell others to go to hell or to say, "Damn you!" which is saying the same thing.

Rather, God warns people of the hell that awaits if they do not repent. We have already seen how this is in the story of Jonah and Nineveh. Jesus, the God-Man, exemplified this too. To warn his audience, he told the parable about Lazarus the beggar and depicts the rich man in the story in hell (Luke 16:19–23). Jesus also warned of the day he would separate the "sheep" and the "goats." These animals are Jesus' metaphors for the redeemed and unredeemed. The "sheep" will inherit eternal life and the "goats" will suffer judgement (Matt. 25:31–46).

The problem remains, nevertheless, as to why God would consign people to ECT. Why not punish them for a limited duration? I would suggest that the endless duration of suffering is due to the unrepentant themselves.

The writer and pastor David Kingdon concludes that sin against God is wrong beyond what we finite beings can conceive.[2] Sin by its nature appears to deserve unending punishment, but it also is possible to escape wholly its power through the salvation offered through Jesus' atoning death. Those who will go to hell are those who refuse salvation and will be incorrigible in this decision. The Bible describes those driven from God's presence as "cowards, traitors, perverts, murderers, the immoral, those who practice magic, those who worship idols, and all liars." (Rev. 21:8.) The nouns used to denote these people suggests that their evildoing is an integral part of their identity which they will not give up. This is not only what they do, but what they are. They practice this sin without a second thought. Their hearts are forever hardened against God. Those who go to hell go because they have chosen their own will in defiance of God's perfect will.

2. Grudem, *Systematic Theology*, 1151.

Religious Pluralism

We obviously live in a pluralistic society where many ethnicities, cultures, and beliefs rub shoulders every day. One way of preserving civil harmony is to emphasize the similarities between what different groups of people believe. This has been sometimes very successful in terms of ethics. The Media does a good job at alerting society to these similarities. For example, we have witnessed how Christians and Muslims have chosen to forgive their persecutors. The Amish community of Nickel Mines in the USA publicly forgave the actions of a mass murderer who opened fire in one of their schools in 2006, killing 5 schoolchildren. Farid Ahmed, a New Zealander Muslim, has forgiven the terrorist who shot his wife in a mass killing in Christchurch in 2019 and is praying for him. Both examples are of extraordinary grace on the part of the bereaved. Both decisions to forgive are the consequence of religious belief. It is in moments of tragedy that people unite to face the circumstances.

However, one of the challenges of a pluralistic society is how to handle the fundamental differences between the truth-claims of religions. Despite the similarities, the very real differences will not go away. The fear is that religious disputes will lead to violence. You might therefore be met with the objection that Christianity is guilty of exclusivity, even hate speech, by saying that Jesus is the only way to salvation. Surely all religions point ultimately in the same direction?

Our response to this matter must be sensitive and intelligent. Implying other people's most fundamental beliefs are false will offend (although some people today seem more than happy to be offensive about Christianity). Moreover, we live in a society where truth has come to mean something personal and individual as much as shared. On this view, we all have our own truths. You have your truth and I have my truth. I will not offend you by challenging your truth and you will not offend me by challenging mine. Of course, there is still a limit to what is acceptable to believe. For example, if I murdered people because I believed an elf had told me to, no right-minded person would accept such a belief.

But asserting that Jesus is the only way is an unfashionable thing at best and deeply offensive at worst. To sustain this claim, we need to do two things: We need to attend to the manner we say it and we need to give reasons why someone ought to embrace Christianity in preference to other worldviews.

First, the manner. According to the apostle Peter, when we give the reasons for our faith, we are to do it "with gentleness and respect." We are to be gentle with people and not preach at them or condemn them. We are to explain patiently the truth to them and invite them to investigate the claims of Christianity further.

Second, what reasons do we have for being confident about recommending Christianity among all faiths and religions to others? We can be assured that we are making no grander claim to know the truth than the person who says that all religions lead to the same God. We seem arrogant by arguing that Jesus is the only way. But to argue that all religions point to the same God is also to make a claim to know the whole truth and that seems no less arrogant.

Christianity is unique in the advantages it possesses over other religions. Its way of salvation is not by having a surplus of good over evil in our deeds account, but by the grace, or undeserved love, of God. This is to our advantage because how do we know if there is more good than bad in our account? What measurement of good and evil do we use? Is a man who commits murder but otherwise lives an exemplary life a worse sinner than someone who spends 20 years pursuing adulterous affairs? Besides, the surplus of good over bad doctrine precludes someone who has been evil all his or her life from receiving salvation at the end of his or her life. If Christianity is exclusivist in that it asserts that Jesus is the only road to salvation, its means of salvation is the most inclusivist of all. In a religion where good deeds must outweigh bad deeds, the naturally better people will have the advantage. Christianity, on the other hand, says that all have sinned and fallen short of the glory of God and that all equally can receive God's gift of salvation.

In a world of immense suffering, Buddhism and Christian Science deal with evil by asserting that it is an illusion. To a father of a terminally ill child, or to a woman who has been beaten and robbed, evil is very real and no pseudo-pious sentiment about evil being unreal will wash. Though we must admit that Christianity appears to have a problem of evil and suffering, the Christian response to evil is the most robust of all religions. Christianity does not deny the reality of evil. Christianity recognizes that evil is as real as goodness. The Christian response goes further to provide a solution to evil and suffering: Salvation from sin and the redemption of the natural order, both achieved by Jesus the God-Man experiencing suffering and evil. No other religion or spiritual worldview claims that God Himself incarnated for human salvation. Only Jesus makes this claim. Christianity is preferable because its God did not stand apart from the world's suffering and evil, but came into the midst of it and suffered more than anyone else ever will.

Christianity is historically reliable in the way no other religion is. Archaeology supports the New Testament record. For example, Roman inscriptions declare that Pontius Pilate and Gallio, the chief magistrate of Corinth before whom Paul was put on trial, exist. The pool called Bethesda in Jerusalem referred to in John 5:2 as a place of healing has been excavated. The New Testament documents can be dated close to the events that they describe which by the historian's criterion of early witness makes them reliable. We have already seen how Paul's First Letter to the Corinthians is dated to the early AD 50s, a mere 20 years after Jesus' death and resurrection, and that it contains a creed that was composed at the start of Christianity. The Gospel of Mark is the earliest of the Gospels, written in the AD 60s. Luke and Matthew's Gospels can be dated to the AD 70s. John's Gospel can be dated to the AD 80s. The historical evidence we have at the start of this book considered for the Resurrection is the best historical evidence for any miracle alleged by any religion.

Islam

Islam is a high-profile religion in contemporary Britain. Despite the vast majority of British Muslims being decent, reasonable people, because of the small extremist minority who have a distorted interpretation of their faith, Islam is associated with terrorist violence unfortunately in the minds of some people. It is important to bear in mind when speaking with Muslims about our faith that we do so on the understanding that many Muslims have endured prejudice and sometimes violence for being Muslims. We must, as the apostle Peter commands us, speak with respect.

To do this, it is important to know first what Muslims believe. In the small space that I have, I cannot do justice to the rich, complex, and diverse nature of Muslim belief and practice. However, I shall attempt to sketch the main outlines of the Islamic religion accurately and fairly in order to facilitate your dialogue with Muslims. To do this, I am drawing on material from a lecture by Mark Ryan who works for *L'Abri* Fellowship International.[3]

To understand Islam, we must understand the prophet, Muhammed, and to understand him, we must understand 7th century Arabia to which he communicated his message. So, we will begin with 7th century Arabia.

Arabia at the time of Muhammed was peopled by herders, farmers, merchants, and raiders. It was a polytheistic culture with different gods and goddesses patronizing individual tribes. Mecca emerged as the chief cultic center where local tribal deities were worshipped. No central authority ruled Arabia. The people were governed in their tribes by elders and chieftains.

It was into this context that Muhammed, the founder and shaper of Islam, was born and raised in Mecca. He developed as an adult the practice of lengthy meditation and in 610 at the age of 40, he began to receive what he regarded as messages from Allah. He continued to receive messages for the next twenty-two years. By 616 AD opposition had manifested among the polytheistic Arabians to Muhammed's message that there was one God. He was

3. Ryan, "An Islam Primer."

resented too for his self-proclamation as a prophet. In 622 AD, Muhammed and his followers left Mecca to escape persecution to live in the city which became known as Medina. Between 622 and 629 AD, Muhammed consolidated the various groups who followed him. During this time, he concluded that Islam was the only revelation that was faithful to Abraham's religion. In 628, after Muhammed's forces had repulsed a Meccan siege of Medina, Muhammed signed a peace treaty with the Meccans which permitted his followers to go on pilgrimage to Mecca. After an attack on the Muslims by Mecca's allies, Muhammed retaliated by capturing Mecca in 630 AD. Eventually, the rest of the Arabian Peninsula submitted to Muhammed. In 632 AD, Muhammed developed a fever and died at the age of 63. Muhammed's achievement at the time of his death had been to unite the Arabian Peninsula as one culture following the laws of Allah.

How do Muslims view Muhammed today? Muslims regard Muhammed not as the founder of Islam, but its reformer. He was chosen to call people out of their idolatry and back to the one God who exists. Muhammed is the model Muslim to be emulated in all aspects of life and his sayings are normative. But he is more than that: He is the last and greatest of all the prophets. Therefore, Muslims do not tolerate any insult aimed at Muhammed. Muhammed is believed to be an intercessor before Allah. Finally, though he is seen as a favored man, Muhammed is not seen as divine.

The *Qur'an* is the sacred book of Islam and without an understanding of it, we cannot understand Islam. Like the Bible, it is used in private devotion and public ceremonies. But in the mind of the Muslim, it is superior to all other sacred texts. According to traditional accounts of the *Qur'an*, it was revealed to Muhammed directly by the angel Gabriel in the Arabic language. But at the time of Muhammed's death, parts of the *Qur'an* had been written down, but much had been committed to memory as was the custom in the oral culture of Arabia. To prevent the loss of the memorized text through the death of the generation that had memorized it, Muhammed's successor Abu Bakr commissioned the process of writing the *Qur'an* down. It is Muslim belief that the *Qur'an* is word for word what Muhammed received from Gabriel and is written in perfect Arabic poetry and prose. It is written mainly in the form of Allah addressing Muhammed.

The central theme of the *Qur'an* is monotheism: The belief that there is one God who is eternal, omnipotent, and omniscient. The second great qur'anic doctrine is its eschatology. The *Qur'an* teaches that there will be a great Day of Judgement in which all humans will be judged by God and divided into those who will enter paradise and those who will suffer in hell. The Day will come suddenly and unexpectedly. Additionally, the *Qur'an* teaches that God has communicated over periods of time via angels with prophets.

It is important to recognize that the *Qur'an* is not the only source of divine guidance for Muslims. The *Sunnah* and *Hadith* provide moral teachings and religious laws to be observed by Muslims. The difference between the two texts is that the *Sunnah* is regarded as wholly inspired whereas the *Hadith* is not.

One way of understanding the essential elements of the Muslim way of life is to know the Five Pillars of Islam. The first pillar is the *Shahada* which is the declaration by which a person becomes a Muslim. It can be translated as: "There is no god but God and Muhammed is God's messenger." The second pillar is *Salah*, or the five daily prayers Muslims say. *Zakat* is charity which consists of spending a portion of one's wealth on the poor and needy. *Sawm* or fasting is the Islamic means of getting close to God. It is obligatory during the period of *Ramadan*. Every Muslim is required to go on pilgrimage to Mecca at least once in his/her lives. This pilgrimage is called the *Hajj*.

A starting point for a discussion with a Muslim could be one of the common grounds between Christianity and Islam. For example, Muslims, like Christians, believe that a final judgement will happen, that people will be bodily resurrected, and either receive the reward of eternal life, or be consigned to hell.

However, such conversations can go only so far before differences emerge. In my interactions with Muslims, their most commonly voiced objections to Christianity are to the doctrine of the Trinity and the identity of Jesus. To Muslims, we are polytheists because we appear to worship three Gods. We also appear idolatrous to them because we consider a man, Jesus, to be God at the same time. How do we answer these objections?

The Trinity does not present three separate gods: Father, Son, and Holy Spirit. That heresy is called Tritheism. Neither are Father, Son, and Holy Spirit different emanations, not persons, of the same substance. That is the heresy called Modalism. What Christianity teaches is that there is one God who has revealed himself in three persons who together make up God.[4]

However, the doctrine of the Trinity is something that is beyond our understanding. It is impossible from our perspective to see how each person of the Trinity can be fully God and yet God is an undivided being. It is important to admit this to our Muslim interlocutors, but not to concede it as a weakness in Christianity. If we were able to understand God fully, God would not be God. God is in part comprehensible otherwise it would be impossible to have a relationship with him. But God is also ineffable because he is an infinite being. It is therefore a sign that we are truly dealing with God when certain things about him are mysterious.

As for the question of Jesus' identity, we can present the case for the Resurrection as an argument for his divinity. We can also present the Trilemma as an argument that Jesus is God in human form.

We can also deal effectively with another Islamic criticism which is the view that the New Testament is riddled with textual errors and therefore is a corrupted text. The accusation that the New Testament is corrupt is not one made by the *Qur'an*. This accusation was first made by the eleventh century Muslim apologist Al-Juwayni. The *Qur'an*, on the other hand, tells Muslims to believe the Gospels (*sura* 5.46). Nowhere in the *Qur'an* are the Christian Scriptures described as corrupt.

4. McDowell, "What is the Trinity?"

Feminism

It is a good thing that we live in a society that legally regards women and men of equal value. This does not always work out in practice, but it is an ideal to which we aspire. A society cannot call itself a civilization if women cannot play their full part in it because of irrational strictures placed on their role.

I say these things as a Christian, but I am aware, and I am sure you are also, that Christianity is seen by secular feminists as a patriarchal religion that seeks to protect the privileges of men at the expense of women. At first glance, it seems very hard to refute these accusations. God is presented as male and the largest Christian denomination, the Roman Catholic Church, refuses to ordain women from among its one billion adherents. Then there are those portions of Scripture that feminists are convinced show that Christianity subjugates females. Wives are instructed by the allegedly misogynistic Paul to submit to their husbands (Eph. 5:22). Paul also commands the Corinthian women to be silent during church meetings for "it is a disgraceful thing for a woman to speak in church" (1 Cor. 14:34–35). How do we demonstrate that Christianity has nothing to fear when it comes to gender equality and that Christianity is a superlative guarantor of the equal status of women?

In refuting the accusation of sexism, it is necessary to go to the beginning of Scripture to see God's ideal. In the first chapter of Genesis, God affirms gender equality:

> 'Then God said, "Let Us make man in Our image, according to Our likeness . . ." So, God created man in His own image, in the image of God He created him; male and female He created them.' (1:26–27)

So far, I have used the *Good News* translation of the Bible, but I have chosen for this quotation the *New King James' Version* as it uses the famous expression, "the image of God". The old-fashioned term man used in this quotation is the generic term for human beings. Man, which is both women and men, is made in God's image. The writer of Genesis' description of the creation of man can be rendered in the following logical form which reveals its egalitarian quality:

1. God made man in His image.
2. Man was created by God as male and female.
3. Therefore, male and female are made in the image of God.

It is astonishing to think that within the context of the ancient Near and Middle East, which was patriarchal, such a text as Genesis 1 emerged.

Eve, the first woman, was given the same responsibility for and authority over the earth as the first man, Adam. It was not the case that Adam was the CEO giving Eve her orders. Both had executive responsibility for this is what God said to both:

> "'Have many children, so that your descendants will live all over the earth and bring it under their control. I am putting you in charge of the fish, the birds, and all the wild animals'" (v. 28).

They had the same job description and I am sure there was no salary distinction in Adam's favor!

Adam and Eve were partners and their partnership is described in additional detail in Genesis 2 in a way that might seem controversial. Eve is referred to as Adam's "helper" (2:18). The word helper might for some people connote the idea that Eve was at Adam's beck and call. Whenever he needed help, he called on Eve who accommodated herself to his needs. But this is not how it should be understood. When a person helps us, they might do this from a position of expertise which we do not have. So, when a businessman goes to see his accountant, she will from the knowledge which she possesses and which he does not have, advise him on his finances. As well as the consultancy role, a helper might have a supervisory role when giving us assistance. If X goes to see his doctor about how to manage his diabetes better, she will help him by exercising a supervisory role over his treatment, diet and lifestyle. Being a helper does not therefore mean having a subordinate role. Instead, it is a role of power and worth.

The role of the helper is also a role that God himself assumes. King David in Psalm 54:4 describes God as his helper. Jesus calls the Holy Spirit "the Helper" (John 15:26). Here the word Helper can be translated also as the Comforter. We therefore never should disdain the role of the helper, whether we be female or male.

But we are all called as Christians to help one another. Men therefore are required to help as much as women. In 1 Corinthians 12:28, Paul describes the roles and gifts that people have within the body of Christ. One of the gifts Paul lists is the gift of helps. This is the gift of being able by the grace of God to provide loving support to others. There is no indication in this text that this gift was solely or mainly given to women.

Where does male domination of women therefore come from? This is a complex anthropological problem for which we do not have the space to evaluate properly. What is important for our present purposes is that if God did not create women to occupy an inferior, exploited, and restricted role, and God does not change, then the subordination of women is a sin and the origin of sin is the human heart. Whatever other explanation we might give for women's subordination, it is an egregious transgression of the law of love. We are to love our neighbors as ourselves (Lev. 19:18; Matt. 5:43). This command is addressed to everyone. Therefore, men are to love women who are their neighbors as themselves. Women are men's neighbors wherever men and women mix. A man's neighbor is his female colleague at work or a fellow student. This is not romantic or sexual love, of course, but a respect and concern for the other's well-being that is modelled on the respect and concern that one has for oneself. To take as an example, if X does not like being interrupted throughout a conversation (I do not think anyone does), then he ought not constantly to interrupt his female colleague, even if she has a quieter, gentler voice than he. Of course, men are to love their male neighbors in this way too and women are obliged to love their male and female neighbors as they do themselves also. Love is meant to be a reciprocal thing among us all and between God and us. As Paul reminded his Roman readers, so we too should "please our brothers and sisters for their own good, in order to build them up in the faith" (15:2).[5]

Part of God's equality is that it is as much about equality of responsibility as it is about opportunity. Women and men are both required to keep God's law perfectly. It is the case that all women and all men are sinful and face the same penalty for failing to do so. As Paul solemnly declares: "everyone has sinned and is far away from God's saving presence" (Rom 3:23). As we read how God's anger against sin leads Him to give the unrepentant over to the consequences of their sinful desires, we see a description of sins for which women and men are equally at fault (Rom 1:18–32). On the Day of Judgment, anyone whose name was not found in the Book of Life was cast into the lake of fire (Rev 20:15). This includes both women and men.

The Good News is that both women and men are saved in the same way from the penalty of their sins and saved in equal measure. As Paul declares: "I have complete confidence in the gospel; it is God's power to save all who believe, first the Jews and also the Gentiles" (Rom 1:16). Women and men are saved for the same reason: Through faith in Jesus Christ who because of the grace of God (the undeserved love of God for sinners), was given as a propitiation, or a sacrificial offering, to take God's wrath which their sins deserve (Rom 3:21–26). There is absolutely nothing in anything Paul wrote that suggests that women and men are not equally saved. Furthermore, women and men are saved to enjoy equally the same enormous benefits of God's salvation. All believers in Christ are freed from the power of sin, are sanctified, and receive the gift of God, which is eternal life (Rom 6:22–23).

In the most essential and significant matters of creation, identity, purpose, and salvation, women and men are equal before God. God is not sexist and neither should His people be. But there is much more we could say on this matter, and as this book is not a book about gender equality but a general introduction to the defense of the faith, may I refer you to chapter seven of an

5. The word 'his' is used by the New King James' traditional language as the generic term for all human beings, both women and men.

excellent book that has already been footnoted: Amy Orr-Ewing's *Why Trust the Bible: Answers to 10 Tough Questions*. That it is a female apologist who has written this chapter is an important consideration for the debate we are discussing.

— 5 —

Conclusion

I HOPE YOU HAVE enjoyed reading this book and that it has given you a firmer understanding of why you believe in Jesus. My thesis has been that the best explanation for the first Easter is the Resurrection of Jesus. To support this thesis and affirm that Jesus was raised by His Father and not a super angel, I have presented signposts that indicate God's existence found in scientific data. I have argued that the creator of the universe and the man who died on the cross are the one and the same person. This book has also provided responses to the problem of evil and suffering and issues that are contemporarily significant. A book of this length cannot answer all the questions and so I have provided a list of resources you may wish to explore in the bibliography and the further reading section. I have also furnished a series of questions that can form the basis of discussion between Christians whose faith is wavering. My book's aim is that you have the reasons for why you believe to hand so that if you do begin to doubt or happen to enter into debate with someone who is not a Christian, you will have a reasonable foundation on which to stand.

At this stage, you may have an unanswered question prompted by the introduction: How did you, Peter Harris, return to your faith? I should very much like to answer this question because it rounds off this text which began with the story of my deconversion and because it might give hope to those who know people who have deconverted that one day they will reconvert and have their relationship with Jesus Christ restored.

Just as my deconversion was a combination of emotional impulses and lines of reasoning, so my reconversion was a combination of feelings and thoughts. I was twenty-seven years old and working as a teacher of English and History in a state secondary school. My life was comfortable: I lived in a pleasant neighborhood, had time often to go to the gym, go out for a drink with friends, and read, write, and publish poetry. But I had reached the point where I was wondering where my life was going. I feared that my life and life *per se* were meaningless. I had no intellectual defense against this conclusion and this conclusion made me fearful.

One day I was standing in my kitchen and I did something I had not done for a long time: I cried out to God, asking Him where my life was headed! Immediately, I began to feel the presence of God again. I had a red pocket Bible which I had never thrown away. I began to read it again. The books of Daniel and Romans became my favorite parts of the Bible. My prayer life which had begun with an existential question soon became deep-felt prayers of repentance for the many wrong things I had said, thought, and done.

God's word had become again a living text rather than a set of untrustworthy documents filled with legends. What shielded me from the doubts about its veracity was a New Testament commentary I found in my local library. I do not remember the name of the book or of the author, but I do remember that the author wrote very intelligently about why the New Testament could be trusted. This was the first apologetic I had ever read and it was very useful in strengthening my recovery from atheism. My prayer is that in some way this book you are now reading helps to sustain your faith, or recover it, or bring someone else to Christ. If it achieves any of those things, I shall be honored.

Further Reference

FOR AN OUTSTANDING AND comprehensive collection of articles defending Christianity and presenting the Christian view on controversial and topical issues, please go to www.bethinking.org. I have already referenced this website in my footnotes and bibliography, but there is so much more to this website. There are many answers to many questions on this site.

I have referenced two of John Lennox's books, but I wish to add a third: His outstanding riposte to New Atheism called *Gunning for God: Why the New Atheists are Missing the Target* (Oxford: Lion, 2011). In fact, read anything on Christianity by John Lennox!

For the question of religious pluralism, I recommend J. P. Moreland's compelling lecture at https://www.bethinking.org/is-christianity-the-only-way/how-do-we-know-christianity-is-right-out-of-all-the-religions.

Concerning Islam, Nabeel Qureshi's text *No God but One: Allah or Jesus?* brilliantly demonstrates that the evidence is very much in Christianity's favor. It was published by Zondervan in 2016.

If you wish to consult a concisely and incisively written book of apologetics regarding Christ, Michael Green's outstanding volume *Jesus for Sceptics* (UCCF: 2013) is exactly that.

The Universities and Colleges' Christian Fellowship has details of the Christian Unions that meet in universities and colleges throughout the UK. Their website is www.uccf.org.uk

If you are looking for a church to attend, https://www.finda-church.co.uk/ is a directory of all churches throughout the UK.

Appendix: Discussion Guide

As we observed in the Introduction, often the church is not good at helping Christians with doubts about the truth of the faith. This discussion guide has been included to stimulate discussion between those who have doubts and those who can help them. The following questions are designed to stimulate that discussion. These are not the only questions that can be asked about the topics that feature in this book and participants in discussions are free to ask different and additional questions to what are listed below.

How discussion groups are set up and run is something that I will not prescribe. It is best that participants decide. There are nevertheless some points of advice I wish to give. I do think that it is important that the church leadership approves of these discussion meetings before they go ahead and that they have some input into their organization. If those involved are minors by law, it is important to have the permission of parents and guardians for their children to take part. If minors and vulnerable adults are present, it is important that the church's safeguarding and child protection policies are adhered to. I would advise that before the discussion session, each participant reads a chapter of the book in the light of the questions to be discussed and their own questions. I think it is also important to pray at the beginning and end of the discussion.

Questions about the Introduction

1. How would you have advised the author, Peter Harris, when he was going through profound doubts about his faith?

2. What is your opinion of Harris' view that the church sometimes does not help doubting Christians well?

3. What could our church do to help doubting Christians better?

4. What makes you doubt?

5. What do you hope to gain from these discussions?

Questions about Chapter One

1. Why does Christianity fail if the Resurrection never happened?

2. Does it surprise you that New Testament scholars, including skeptical ones, can agree on five facts? Be prepared to explain your answer.

3. Which natural explanation for the Resurrection do you find the weakest and why?

4. Which natural explanation for the Resurrection do you find the strongest? How well does Harris deal with this explanation?

5. Harris argues that the Resurrection alone cannot prove the existence of God, for a super being could have raised Jesus. What do you think of his argument?

Questions about Chapter Two

1. How do you view the relationship between the Christian faith and science? Has reading this book changed your view and if so, why?

APPENDIX: DISCUSSION GUIDE

2. Would you use the kalam cosmological argument as a reason for God's existence? Explain your response.

3. What is your opinion of the argument for God's existence from fine-tuning?

4. Is it possible to be a theistic evolutionist and a Christian?

5. What is your understanding of the statement that humans are made in the image of God?

Questions about Chapter Three

1. How strong is Habermas' view that the Scriptures are reliable?

2. Is the Trilemma a good argument for Jesus' divine nature?

3. After reading this chapter, do you think you can assert confidently that miracles can happen?

4. What in your opinion is the best Christian response to the problem of evil?

5. And what in your opinion is the best Christian response to the problem of suffering?

Questions about Chapter Four

1. How would you respond to the question, who made God?

2. Is the doctrine of hell as eternal conscious punishment an embarrassment for Christians?

3. What would you say to a religious pluralist who says that all religions lead to God?

4. What is the best response to a Muslim who does not accept that Jesus was the Son of God?

5. What do you think of the view that a person cannot be a Christian and a feminist at the same time?

Bibliography

Barton, Karl. "The History of the Liar, Lunatic, Lord Trilemma." https://conversantfaith.com/2012/05/04/the-history-of-liar-lunatic-lord-trilemma/.

Bruce, F. F. *The Book of the Acts*. Grand Rapids: Eerdmans, 1988.

Cavin, Robert Greg. "Miracles, Probability, and the Resurrection of Jesus." PhD diss., University of California-Irvine, 1993.

Cicero, Marcus Tullius. *Against Verres*, 2.5.165. http://perseus.uchicago.edu/perseus-cgi/citequery3.pl?dbname=PerseusLatinTexts&getid=1&query=Cic. Ver. 2.5.165.

Coulter, Paul. "Let There Be Light: Illuminating the Creation / Evolution Debate." https://www.bethinking.org/does-evolution-disprove-creation/let-there-be-light.

Craig, William Lane. "The Kalam Cosmological Argument." https://www.reasonablefaith.org/writings/popular-writings/existence-nature-of-god/the-kalam-cosmological-argument/.

———. "The Problem of Evil." https://www.bethinking.org/suffering/the-problem-of-evil.

Crossan, John Dominic. *Jesus: A Revolutionary Biography*. New York: HarperCollins, 1994.

Dawkins, Richard. *River Out of Eden*. High Wycombe: Phoenix, 1995.

———. *The God Delusion*. London: Black Swan, 2007.

———. "The God Delusion (Full Documentary)." https://www.youtube.com/watch?v=RHAz-ULSdhI.

Dirckx, Sharon. *Am I Just My Brain?* Epsom: The Good Book, 2019.

———. *Why? Looking at God, evil & personal suffering*. Nottingham: InterVarsity, 2013.

Groothuis, Douglas. *Christian Apologetics: A Comprehensive Case for Biblical Faith*. Downers Grove, IL.: InterVarsity, 2011.

Grudem, Wayne. *Systematic Theology: An Introduction to Biblical Doctrine*. InterVarsity: Leicester, 2000.

Habermas, Gary R. "Recent Perspectives on the Reliability of the Gospels." https://www.bethinking.org/is-the-bible-reliable/recent-perspectives-on-the-reliability-of-the-gospels.

————. *The Historical Jesus.* Joplin, MO: College, 1996.

Habermas, Gary R., and Licona, Michael R. *The Case for the Resurrection of Jesus.* Grand Rapids, MI: Kregel, 2004.

Hazen, Craig. "Evidence for the Resurrection." Module One Lecture for Biola University's Certificate in Apologetics.

Hedley Brooke, John. *Science and Religion: Some Historical Perspectives.* Cambridge: Cambridge University Press, 2014.

Hitchens, Christopher. *God is Not Great: How Religion Poisons Everything.* London: Atlantic, 2007.

Jackson, Frank. "What Mary Didn't Know." *Journal of Philosophy* 83 (5 May 1986) 291–95.

Lennox, John. *God's Undertaker: Has Science Buried God?* Oxford: Lion, 2009.

————. *Seven Days That Divide The World: The Beginning According to Genesis and Science.* Grand Rapids: Zondervan, 2011.

Licona, Mike, R. "Jesus - The Son of Man?" https://www.bethinking.org/jesus/jesus-the-son-of-man.

May, Peter. "What is the Image of God." https://www.bethinking.org/human-life/what-is-the-image-of-god.

Josh McDowell Ministry. "Did Jesus really claim to be God?" https://www.bethinking.org/jesus/q-did-jesus-really-claim-to-be-god.

MacDowell, Josh. "What is the Trinity? Do Christians worship three gods?" https://www.bethinking.org/god/q-what-is-the-trinity-do-christians-worship-three-gods.

Meyer, Stephen, "DNA and Other Things." *First Things* April 2000.

Orr-Ewing, Amy, *Why Trust the Bible: Answers to 10 Tough Questions.* Nottingham: InterVarsity, 2005.

Owen, Coleman, et al. "Detecting Awareness in the Vegetative State." *Science* 313.5792 (September 2006) 1402.

Premier Radio. "Unbelievable? John Lennox vs Peter Atkins - Can Science Explain Everything? Live Debate." https://www.premierchristianradio.com/Shows/Saturday/Unbelievable/Episodes/Unbelievable-John-Lennox-vs-Peter-Atkins-Can-Science-Explain-Everything-Live-Debate.

Than, Ker. "Humans add to natural disaster risk." http://www.nbcnews.com/id/9731968/ns/technology_and_science-science/t/humans-add-natural-disaster-risk/#.XPlF1ExFzIU.

Ward, Keith. *Why There Almost Certainly Is a God: Doubting Dawkins.* Oxford: Lion, 2008.

Yancey, Philip. "Faith and Doubt." https://philipyancey.com/q-and-a-topics/faith-and-doubt.

Index

abductive argument, 33
Abu Bakr, 59
Adam, 48–49, 63
Adam and Eve, 24, 48
aesthetic sense, of humans, 30
Ahmed, Farid, forgave a terrorist, 55
Alexander the Great, 6
Alien Theory, for the Resurrection, 5, 10
Al-Juwayni, on the New Testament as corrupt, 61
Allah, 59, 60
Amish community, forgave a mass murderer, 55
animals, 29, 30–31
apologetics, regarding Christ, 69
Aquinas, Thomas, xiv
Arabia, at the time of Muhammed, 58
archaeology, supporting the New Testament record, 57
Aristotle, anthropomorphic assumption, 20
atheists, xiv, 23, 46–47
Atkins, Peter, 13
author, return to faith of, 67–68

Bach, Johann Sebastian, xiv
beauty, appreciation of, 30

Behe, Michael, 24, 25, 32
Bethesda pool, in Jerusalem, 57
bethinking.org website, 69
biblical kind, corresponding to species, 26
biological life, basis of, 33
biological reproduction, scientific truths of, 45
Blakemore, Colin, 18
bodily resurrection, of Jesus, 3
brain, as a machine, 18
brain-imaging techniques, on vegetative patients, 19
Brooke, John Hedley, 14
Buddhism, on evil as illusion, 57

category mistake, on God as a caused being, 51
cause to the universe, asserting, 16–20
cell, complex parts of a single, 32
Certificate in Apologetics, 5n7
Chalmers, David, 19
change, God as the author of profound, 29
Christian Science, dealing with evil as illusion, 57
Christian Unions, throughout the UK, 69

Mark (Gospel of), as the earliest of
the Gospels, 57
materialists, on morality as part of
evolution, 34
mathematics, describing the
universe, 21
May, Peter, 28–31
Mecca, 58
Merton, R. K., 14
Merton Thesis, 14
Messiah, Son of Man as, 38
Meyer, Stephen, 33
mind(s)
creating order, 20
of God as independent of brains,
17
as independent of and beyond
the brain, 18
loving God with, xv
nature of, 17
pre-existing the universe, 19
skeptical, 6
Minimal Facts Approach, to the
Resurrection, 2–4
miracles, 39–41
Modalism, as heresy, 61
monotheism, of Islam, 60
morality, 30–31, 34
Moreland, J. P., 69
Morris, Simon Conway, 25
Muhammed, 58, 59
multiverse theory, 23
Muslims, 55, 58, 59
mutations, as usually harmful,
27–28
myth, explaining scriptures as, 24

natural disasters, 47, 48
natural explanations, 4–6
natural order, to be healed by God,
49
natural reason, for the first Easter,
12
natural selection, 23–24, 28

natural world, 47
naturalism, 42
Neanderthals, 28
neuroscience, 19
New Age beliefs, 31
New Atheism, 13
new heaven and a new earth, 29
New Testament, 36–37, 61, 68
Ninevites, God warning of
impending judgement, 52
No God but One: Allah or Jesus?
(Qureshi), 69
"no-body" theory, of the
Resurrection, 3
non-existence, 53
non-material cause, of the universe,
15
non-reductive materialism, 18
nothing, universe emerging out
of, 15
nuclear DNA, 33

observable universe, 22
Occam's Razor, 23
order, minds creating, 20
organisms, seeming to be mutation-
averse, 27
Orr-Ewing, Amy, 66
Owen, Adrian, 19

pain, problem of, 43, 46–49
paleontology, 26
partnership, of Adam and Eve, 63
Passover Plot, for the Resurrection,
5, 9–10
Paul
acted on the Sanhedrin's behalf,
9
became a follower of Jesus, 11
believed he saw Jesus alive, 8
commanded Corinthan women
to be silent, 62
conversion of, 4, 41
on God's power to save all, 65

Lightning Source UK Ltd.
Milton Keynes UK
UKHW021859051122
411712UK00009B/369